AMERICAN NOMADS:
HOW TO FIND + RENT TO
THE REMOTE WORKER

AMERICA'S NEW TENANT CLASS IS HERE TO STAY

ERIN SPRADLIN

.thank you.

*To my husband, James: you are a wonderful human being.
Thank you for your editing help, consistent support, and
friendship. I love you.*

Table of Contents

A Letter to The Reader

Dear Reader,

Thank you for picking up this book. Double thank you for buying it. To help you understand what to expect from *American Nomads*, I've put together a quick overview of topics the book will cover.

The philosophy underlying *American Nomads:*
- COVID-19 forced nearly all professional positions to go remote
- there are a lot of economic incentives for employers to keep employees remote
- the number of full-time remote workers has grown and will continue to grow
- now that employees are remote workers, they can live anywhere
- many remote workers will try out different places to live
- remote workers often make great tenants
- remote workers can be your tenants if you know what they need and how to find them
- I'm the person to tell you how to do that because I have experience with this

Who should read *American Nomads*:
This book is for people who want to learn the following information about remote workers:

- who they are
- what they require
- how to find them
- what types of properties they are most likely to rent

Why I Wrote the Book
In my opinion, real estate education needs to (1) address current trends in a timelier fashion and (2) recognize and speak to the young, hesitant, or intimidated (but real estate curious) audience. In a perfect world, real estate would have a more diverse set of participants and cater to a larger audience.

My hope for my real estate career and for this book is to make real estate education and real estate investing more accessible.

Because I believe remote workers are an emerging tenant class similar to Airbnb-ers, with a lot of upside potential and growth, this seemed like a good place to address current trends and speak to people who may not naturally see themselves as investors.

Two weeks before the completion of this book, Airbnb released its Airbnb 2021 revamp. Some of the most major added functionality supports 28+ day stays. Airbnb's CEO, Brian Chesky, explained the decision this way: "In 2019, 14% of our guests stayed for 28+ days. In 2021, the number is 24%. I do not think this trend is going away."[i] What features did they add? You'll have to read the book to find out.

After the book

If you want more content on this topic, I recommend visiting our website: www.AmericanNomadsBook.com. Our website has a guide for renting to remote workers, as well as articles and videos on the topic. If that doesn't do it for you, please email me at erin@American No-madsBook.com. I write back. I promise!

Thank you again,
Erin Spradlin

Intro | The Future is Here

I was waiting in the car for my husband in late October 2020 when I read an NPR article[ii]about remote workers that blew my mind. For you, dear reader, I distill the highlights:

- 14-23 million Americans plan to relocate now that they are no longer tethered to their jobs
- many companies are planning on making the work-from-home trend a permanent fixture
- people want to move to places they can afford and/or where they want to live
- there has been a 32% uptick in people's interest in moving

And here's some more interesting information about remote workers from the website Any Place

- traveling remote workers have grown by 49% since 2019
- the remote workforce has grown 140% since 2005:[iii]

Finally, a Harris poll revealed that 40% of Americans want to stay remote permanently, while 35% want a hybrid model and 25% want to return to the office full time.[iv]

Here's what I think you should care about: Remote workers existed before but made up a very small population (approximately five million Americans). Because of COVID-19, that number has recently exploded. And because some people can work from anywhere now, it seems like a lot more of them will be doing just that. Some of them will be buying and some will be renting. Those who are renting will need somewhere to live. *American Nomads* is about finding remote workers and renting to them.

Lest you think it's just me and NPR that believe this, Zillow and FlexJobs are also reporting and paying attention to this trend.

Zillow calls this the "Great Reshuffling" and describes the participating population as "those able to move from location to location, staying connected to work and family digitally, while experiencing new adventures in unfamiliar destinations. Whether looking for a new city or town to experience for one month or six months, digital nomads may be exploring various locations in hopes of eventually making a permanent move."[v] I am calling this trend American Nomadism and encouraging you to consider this your lucrative rental future.

Flexobs cites an Upwork study which estimates that by 2025, 22% of the US workforce will be working remotely.[vi]

As of late June 2021, Airbnb has added filters and additions to its website to support this trend. Of all the companies and media outlets paying attention, it's Airbnb that I care most about. They are a forward-thinking company that has been in this space for some time. Previously, Airbnb was there in a limited capacity because the demand was limited; their adjustment signals this trend is about to explode. Airbnb has added a special section for 28+ day rentals and is advising hosts to "harness a growing trend." They are reporting more than a 50% increase internationally for longer stays and a 30% increase in growth in the United States as of September 2020.[vii]

As of May 2021, when this book was being processed for its final edit, Airbnb had partnered with Tulsa Remote (more about Tulsa Remote later) and was reporting that 47% of Americans were interested in "trying before buying" in a new city. To meet this demand, Airbnb launched an entire program around 28+ day stays to help people explore before commit-ting.[viii]

Shortly after the "try before you buy" launch, Airbnb also added incredible flexibility in their filter function. People searching for Airbnbs are no longer limited by time, dates, or destination. People who want to live whenever and wherever because they no longer have geographic job descriptions and want to get out of town can just find somewhere to go. Will all these people be 28+ day travelers? The number of long-term travelers will still be lower than short-term travelers, but again, this flex power suggests that Airbnb believes remote work is here to stay and growing fast. The redesign is all about catering to the future of remote employment.

Back in the car that day in October, the NPR article confirmed everything I already believed: employers will be disincentivized to bring workers back given the cost of commercial real estate, which means many people won't need to be close to their jobs now or in the future. Some portion of those professionals will want to try living in another location if they are no longer geographically tied to their jobs. Everything I've researched in the past six months has only reinforced my belief that this trend is here and growing rapidly.

Big picture: we are in the middle of a relocation revolution that has the potential to grow in the near and long-term future. As a landlord who needs tenants in a state that is attractive to visitors (Colorado), this trend is personally interesting to me. And on a professional level, as a real estate agent with investor clients, I believe this is a trend that everyone can and should get excited about.

By the time my husband returned to the car last October, I had decided to write this book because it seemed clear that remote workers were disrupting the United States housing and rental market, and I believe they will continue to do so.

I think you may share my view or are curious about my view if you fit one of the following descriptions:

- you own a rental property
- you are considering owning a rental property

- you are enjoying or have enjoyed the extra cash afforded to you through Airbnb hosting
- you would like to reduce the cost of your existing mortgage

If the above rings true, you need to start studying remote workers as much as I do. This book is a great place to start because it will tell you:

- who these remote workers are
- what these remote workers want
- what kind of property suits remote workers best
- how to outfit an existing rental or portion of your house to cater to remote workers
- how to find remote worker tenants.

.a word about definitions.

Being confused isn't that fun when you are driving on the interstate, have a peanut allergy, or are making a major real estate decision. This table is here to help illustrate some important definitions before we start.

	Other Names	Furnished?	Rental Length
Short-term rental (STR)	Airbnb, VRBO	Yes	Less than a month
* Medium-term rental	American Nomadism, remote-worker model, digital nomadism, subletting, 30+ day furnished model, traveling nurse model, corporate model	Yes	30+ days or more *Note, while Brian Chesky comments that 25% of the stays are 28 days or more, most city laws stipulate rentals should be 30+ days. Make your option 30+ days to protect yourself.
Long-term rental	Traditional rental model, renters	No	Usually 6 months or more

* I have highlighted and added asterisks to the medium-term rental model definition because the model is the focus of this book.

.chapter one.

The Future

***

- 33% of the US workforce is remote working[ix]
- 66% of remote workers do not want to return to the office[x]

Implications for the boss

Yes, we must start here. If you are a part-time landlord (meaning you invest but still work full time) or have friends or family or lovers that have bosses, you may have noticed they have an outsized importance, so we have to figure out their current and long-term motivations. Will bosses be motivated to bring people back into the office or not?

There are two types of bosses: Futurists and Boss Dinosaurs.

You don't really need to worry about Futurists because Futurist Bosses are known for embracing technology and being forward thinking. Airbnb CEO Brian Chesky is a Futurist. Brian Chesky not only had the idea for Airbnb, he can also see that a major change for business travel is on the horizon/already here, "If you think about where business travel is going in the future, it seems completely intuitive to me that as companies offer more flexibility, more people are going to live around the world, but they're not all going to want to live remote," he explained in *Business Travel News*. "They're going to have to come back to visit, and so I think you're going to start to see longer stays. ... You're going to see longer stays going in cities. We're seeing elevated bookings in urban markets for stays of longer than 28 days." He went on to add that stays of 28+ days were up 24% from 14% in 2019.[xi]

You never need to explain to Futurists the importance of social media, or that a phone book is basically just a tree-killing doorstop at this point, because your boss already got that. Your boss might still not understand TikTok, but they gave you the green light on utilizing the platform to generate business. Futurist bosses may have already implemented measures to facilitate partial remote work, and may be open to full-time remote work. Futurist bosses recognize full-time remote work is coming and they aren't fighting it.

Boss Dinosaurs are also affectionately called Luddites. These are bosses that previously refused to embrace remote work because they don't totally understand it, can't trust it, and feel most comfortable with forty hours in-house. Your standard *butts-in-seats* model is what they know and like.

Since March 2020, both Futurists and Boss Dinos have received an enormous amount of new data on how remote workers perform. Futurists are probably reading articles on it from their new solar-powered home in a tree they've named Lola in a Peruvian forest, whereas

Boss Dinos are sending telegrams across the country with the words "It's possible I was wrong when I rejected advances in technology." Boss Dinos have this new attitude because the work they oversaw has not suffered lapses in productivity since COVID-19 started.

Now is a good time to tattoo this onto your brain: many companies have gained financially by sending their workforce home. To begin, employees are more productive (this study[xii] estimates that remote workers are actually 1.4 days per week more productive than their in-house peers, which translates to three extra weeks of work per year.) Second, empty offices no longer need to supply snacks, computers, desk phones, offices, electricity, plumbing, or most expensive: office space. Aside from saving all that overhead, you may also start saving on staff if you are getting 28% more work out of the same worker. In fact, that could mean you need 28% fewer employees.

Because many businesses exist for only one reason ($$$), employers will be financially incentivized to keep their workforce remote. And those that bring their staff back to the office may be forced to adopt a more lenient remote work policy now that the pandemic has proven remote work can be done effectively. Added to that, as of December 2020, Fortune Magazine reports 33% of workers do not want to return to the office.[xiii] Most companies don't have the luxury to alienate 33% of the available workforce, and the companies that do have that luxury, won't.[xiv] What I mean by that is, Facebook could require a blood sacrifice as the price of admission and people would still want to work there, but in the future they won't be requiring employees to be in office. Facebook is preparing for a future that supports a 50% remote workforce. Is Facebook doing this to be generous? Maybe, but it seems more likely that Facebook wants to be able to select from the best talent pool, and they understand that means allowing for remote work.[xv]

There are implications for a full remote workforce. The motivation behind it helps us to understand the future size and importance of remote workers as they expand the tenant pool.

Implications for the employee

There are a lot of implications for the employee, especially if they have children, but the main points in this book are the remote worker's abilities to work from anywhere now, and what environment will be needed to support working from home.

People have a lot of reasons to move. Some of the more popular reasons listed are traffic, cost of living, terrible weather, isolation, desire to be closer to families, etc. Some of the less popular reasons are: wanting to try a different city, dreams of living near a beach/mountains/on the East Coast, etc. Later in the book, we'll discuss when and if those reasons matter, but at this point, what matters most is that a lot of people now have the ability to work from anywhere. And of that group, some of them want to move. And of *that* group, some of them want to rent in a new location before committing (that's where you come in).

1	Closer to friends and family	31%
2	Affordable living	27%
3	Job relocation	21%
4	More space	18%
5	Ability to work from anywhere	17%
6	Different climate	17%[xvi]

The other implication for the employee is finding an office in the absence of having an office. For most people, this means transforming a space in their primary residence to allow them to work. Whether that's the primary residence they own or the one they rent from you, there are ways to make home spaces productive, professional spaces.

Implications for the tenant

The main implication for the tenant is that they can actually become tenants.

As the NPR story mentioned above points out, when freed up geographically from their jobs, a ton of people want to live somewhere else. They no longer have to live somewhere with terrible weather, limited culture, or a proximity that is far too close (or not close enough) to family. They no longer have to pay steep rent or mortgages to be close to their jobs. They can move across the country to live near family. They can live in a mountain town and ski most mornings. Basically, if there is an upside to COVID-19, for many people it is being free to live wherever they want because they no longer have to live near their work.

My assumption about this new class of tenant, this "American Nomad" (heretofore interchangeably called the "remote worker"), who can and has decided to uproot their lives and move elsewhere, is that they will be moving with a mixture of joy and caution. Like all groups, they are not a monolith and will approach trying out a new city one of two ways: first, as excited pioneers ready to put down roots, and second, as reluctant adventurers ("reluctants").

It's the latter group you care about: the reluctants. Reluctants may have been living a life they weren't particularly satisfied with for a long time and feel the need for a change. They are not looking to marry themselves to something else immediately. They want to explore. They want to play the field. They want to make sure the fit is right. Perhaps they rushed in last time and are not eager to do so now.

Cool, but what are you even talking about, Erin? Are we talking about dating now? I thought this was a real estate strategy book. What I'm saying is, in my experience, tenants that decide to resettle elsewhere have left a situation where they are less than fully satisfied and don't want to repeat the mistake. For that reason, they are much more likely to want to dip their toe into a new city before committing. Reluctants want to try before they buy. Reluctants are renters. And that is why we care about reluctants.

Implications for the landlord

It's time to rethink what being a landlord means. Traditionally, landlords have rented you an unfurnished place for six months to a year. Since the emergence of Airbnb in 2008 (and from the time it became a force to be reckoned with: 2014), many people have dabbled in Airbnb rentals (aka, short-term rentals). Short-term rentals are furnished homes that are typically booked for shorter stints (between one day to one week, usually). While Airbnb turned vacationing and accommodations upside down, it turned property investing on its head as well. I know this because it allowed me to quit the job I hated in 2016, inspired me to go into real estate full time in 2017, and I spent the first two years of my career trying to help people understand: this does work. It isn't a scam, and short-term rental money is much, much better than a long-term rental. So, Airbnb changed things. It changed things for the better for people who were early adopters of new technology and investing models. And now, yet another new investing model is here: the remote worker rental model.

Remote workers are going to be a new tenant class. They are going to be a lucrative tenant class. And you should start thinking about the remote worker renter and what they want. Now.

Part I | Profile of the Worker

While the target audience of this book is landlords, I am doing an overview of who the remote worker is because as your future tenants, they are your new customers. Successful businesses know their customers—who are they and what do they want? A successful landlord should have the same interest in their tenants. For that reason, the first part of this book will speak to who the tenant is and what motivates them.

.chapter two.
Remote Workers: Who Are They?

We don't know everything about who remote workers are yet because we've never had a pandemic that geographically liberated people quite the way COVID-19 has. That said, remote workers have an ancestor of sorts: the digital nomad. Digital nomads were the first remote workers, and we should look to them as a reasonable model for the future.

Digital Nomads + Remote Workers

The term digital nomad[xvii] first showed up in 1997. However, like Airbnb, the trend gained popularity in 2014 (apparently, 2014 was a cool, fun, and forward-thinking year. Kudos to you, '14). Digital nomadism just means that people work remotely. Their digital devices allow them to be nomadic. For the American traveler, this meant that many of them moved overseas to affordable and beautiful destinations. Thailand, Portugal, Colombia, and Mexico were popular hotspots for nomadism as they all had fantastic weather, the infrastructure to support working abroad, were cost-effective, and friendly to the nomad lifestyle.

Let's stop for a second to point out a few important differences between digital nomads and remote workers.

First, unlike digital nomads, most remote workers did not proactively seek out remote work or build a life around remote work, but were thrust into it in March 2020. Digital nomads are people (US citizens and other nationalities) that have proactively sought out careers and lifestyles that allow them to travel the world. Digital nomads are driven by adventure more than they are driven by careers.

While some remote workers may also be travel motivated, a much larger portion of them are predominantly career driven. And since COVID-19 forced the remote work experiment, they plan on taking advantage of their geographic freedom now.

Second, remote workers are probably US citizens who choose to stay and travel in the United States. The remote worker may want an adventure without wanting the effort and expense of an international adventure. For these reasons, even as vaccines become widely available, the United States is set to see a lot of movement within its own borders.

Third, remote workers have gender and age diversity similar to high-skill professionals. Again, this is because COVID-19 forced the experiment on us. For that reason, the pool of remote workers likely reflects the pool of high-skill workers. Further, within that group, there is a subset of corporate professionals that have jobs that can be done entirely remotely. This subset actually makes up about 20% of the overall American labor force and is more prevalent in advanced economies than emerging economies. Certain industries have more positions that require no in-person collaboration. Finance, insurance, management, and business services are all industries that have a higher pool of workers who can work remote full time.[xviii]

Who opts to travel of this more diversified population is still emerging, and will change as the practice becomes more common, but the demographic base of the US remote worker is more diverse than the demographic base of the US digital nomad.

When thinking about who the remote worker is, it's fair to assume they are a blend of digital nomads and high-skill workers.

Income

As of April 2021, ZipRecruiter reports the average income of United States remote workers is $66,180 annually.[xix] After taxes, that's roughly $50,000 take-home. Monthly take-home averages out to $4,000.

The 30% rule says to keep your rent expenses below 30%[xx] of your income, which would put your average renter at $1,800-ish. The upper 75th percentile of remote workers makes on average $93,500 and the upper 90th percentile averages $120,000.[xxi]

Annual	Monthly	Available for Monthly Rent (30%)
$66,000	$4,000	$1,250.00
$93,500	$5,616	$1,800.00
$120,000	$7,100	$2,100.00
$250,000	$20,833	$6,249.00[xxii]

Since this is a model, it's a generalization that may not fully reflect reality or make total sense. To begin with, a lot of American renters spend between 30-50% of their income on rent. Additionally, the model doesn't consider that people who have paid off student debt or don't have children may have more disposable income, and thus, more funds for rent.

According to MakeMyMove, a website dedicated to crafting offers for remote workers (more on that in a bit), remote workers have high salaries and often come out of technology, marketing, and sales—although Make-MyMove is quick to point out that the appeal of remote work is not limited to these fields.[xxiii]

Gender

According to *Anyplace*, men predominantly make up the digital nomad landscape, as it is males that make up nearly 70% of nomads, while women make up 30%.[xxiv] What this means in a nutshell is that, as a landlord interested in this model, men are your target audience.

While I previously mentioned that there will be more gender diversity among remote workers, that diversity will likely mirror corporate America. When looking at corporate work in America, gender was divided the following ways:

- entry level: 53% male, 47% female
- managerial: 62% male, 38% female
- senior manager/director: 67% male, 33% female
- vice president: 71% male, 29% female

- senior vice president: 72% male, 28% female
- c-suite: 79% male, 21% female[xxv]

Looking at these numbers, we know that senior corporate positions skew more toward men. Men and women gain these positions as they get more experience in their careers, and thus are older. Since we know Americans are having babies later in life, we can assume this happens on a parallel track with professionals starting to advance their careers into more senior positions. Likewise, we also know that during this time, women have children and their careers are often impacted (and, yes, that sucks, and no, I'm not going to talk about it more than that).

The reason we care about economic advancement and growth of the family is because the bulk of traveling remote workers (American Nomads) will not be moving around with families. From the list with the gender breakdown of different corporate positions, we should assume the bulk of the remote work tenant base will be people with entry level, managerial, and senior managerial careers. They all still skew toward being male, with a more significant divide showing up at the managerial level. Rough numbers here, 60% of the high-skill population likely to do remote work is male.

Will the gender balance change for remote workers? Men are more willing to take chances (Don't get mad at me; data backs this up. Data also supports the notion that the best decisions are made when both men and women are involved, but while encouraging, that's not what this paragraph is about). Men make riskier financial investments, assume they can take leadership positions, and might be more open to traveling the world.[xxvi] Because of this comfort with risk, it makes sense that men would be more open to international travel, which can feel like a huge leap. While domestic travel also has risks, these may feel smaller, and therefore more women may enter this pool. There is a difference between someone feeling bored and motivated to try something new, versus someone who wants to sell everything, fly twenty hours across the world, and settle in a village with a different language, different currency, and different foods. That's a bigger risk and larger mindset shift than American Nomadism. American Nomadism will look more like someone leaving Minneapolis's harsh climate in winter to try out beach living in Southern California for two months. For that reason, American Nomads will likely have more female adherents than digital nomads do.

Because American Nomadism is still in its infancy, we may not have these numbers for another couple years, but I think the gender trends in nomadism will be worth revisiting. Since an influx of females into American Nomadism may or may not happen, I recommend that we continue to view males as our target demographic, and females as a subset.

Men generally have lower expectations for their rental space,[xxvii] are less concerned with physical assaults and burglaries,[xxviii] and may care more about access to sporting events, cable with sporting events, and proximity to bars and nightlife.

Your female subset also enjoys socializing, *but* more than that, they care about rentals that are aesthetically pleasing,[xxix] safe,[xxx] and have quick and easy access to other humans (ladies are more social,[xxxi] and they may want to be closer to coworking spaces).

We'll do a deeper dive on that, but it's important to note because there are differences. Your space may dictate who your rental will appeal to and at what cost. For instance, if you have a darkly-lit basement unit where you have to park in the back and access through a sketchy stairwell, it is more likely your target tenant will be male versus female.

Relationships + Children

In the past, digital nomadism required people who had jobs that could accommodate remote work, and often a wildly different time zone, which limited business calls, etc., in real time. Securing a job with this set of criteria is challenging enough for one person, let alone two.

That said, remote workers in the continental United States have a different situation.

To begin with, COVID-19 forced remote work as an experiment. I mentioned Boss Dinosaurs above, and I'll mention them again. Boss Dinosaurs were resistant to remote work and kept staff in-house, and consequently, geographically close to their jobs. COVID-19 forced Boss Dino hands, allowed for remote work, and in many cases probably proved that not only can remote workers survive, they can also thrive (remember, they are 13% more productive than their in-house peers). Additionally, not paying for utilities, expensive commercial space, and maintaining in-house equipment saves companies a lot of money.

One consequence of COVID-19 is that we likely have a larger demographic of couples where both partners can do their jobs remotely and are no longer tethered to their workplaces. That in itself is going to create a much larger pool of American Nomads.

In the past, a small subset of digital nomads traveled with their children, homeschooled their children, and explored a non-traditional lifestyle. For the most part though, the number of people traveling part or full time with children was limited for several reasons. These include, but are not limited to, the desire to keep kids in a good school district near their friends and in established schedules.

Many of these concerns persist with or without COVID-19. My clients and friends who are parents have told me that the future of school remains uncertain. When schooling was interrupted, a lot of parents had to adopt some form of home schooling, either formally or informally. Some of these parents are more open to remote learning now, knowing what that experience looks like. For this reason, there will be a slight increase in American Nomads traveling with children, but I contend this demographic will remain quite small, as the need to keep kids in routines and near friends and family will likely supersede the desire to travel.

However, again, if you have a property that caters to American Nomads with children, lean into that. People traveling with children are a niche demographic and will likely pay extra for kid-friendly accommodations.

Like all good marketing strategies, there's money in not being the service or property for everyone, but being the service and property that specializes for a subset.

Age

The average age of the digital nomad is thirty-eight.

The average life expectancy in seventeenth-century England was thirty-nine.[xxxii] That number is misleading though, because about 25% of the population died in childhood, including 12% in the first year and 60% (yes, sixty freaking percent) by the age of sixteen, which as you can imagine, brings the overall number down. For people who survived childhood, the average lifespan was fifty-nine.

Similar to the seventeenth-century life expectancy, I believe the average age of digital nomads is misleading because this statistic reflects large populations of young and older people in the pool. Is the true age of a digital nomad thirty-eight, or is it that you have large populations who are younger (not career focused yet) and large populations in post-retirement?

While the website Krisp says the average age is thirty-eight,[xxxiii] with 54% of the nomad population being older than that and millennials only comprising a mere 27%, the *Digital Nomad Survival Guide*[xxxiv] seems to think the concentration is between twenty-four and thirty-four years old.

A Bankrate.com survey supports the idea that the pandemic migration skews younger. During the pandemic, some 31% of people aged eighteen to thirty-one moved for an extended period of time, or permanently.[xxxv] A deeper dive further demonstrates that the young are open to change: 32% of Gen Z, ages eighteen to twenty-four, moved, and 26% of millennials, ages twenty-five to forty, moved.

Distilling this down, your target demographic is people eighteen to forty years of age.

If your rental strategy is to focus on a demographic subset, then make sure you know and love that niche. What does the 50+ niche care about? What does the twenty-five-and-under niche care about? I can and will outline some of these preferences below, but my core advice is: do what you know. If you are forty, you probably have the best sense of what is going on right now for forty-year-olds, with or without kids. You'll naturally have a better understanding of what that demographic wants. Likewise, if you are thirty, target the thirty-and-under set, as that is a time in your life that presents unique freedoms, and you will have a better understanding of what they want.

Education

Unsurprisingly, remote workers are pretty well educated. According to the *Digital Nomad Survival Guide*, 55% of them are college educated while another 28% have completed their masters. International nomads are often attracted to the lifestyle because it is cost effective.

Digital nomadism has not been limited to the uber wealthy. That said, there is an inherent assumption of comfort (often supported by personal wealth or families with enough wealth) that allows for risk taking.

This demographic is large enough, and likely homogenous enough, for me to encourage you to cater to the educated. Since we know educated people could have studied many different topics, I wouldn't go crazy trying to meet their specific interests...*but*, I probably would keep a decent library on site. Would I spend a lot on it? Nope. I'd buy that bookshelf from IKEA or get it from Goodwill, and I'd also get the books from a thrift store or a used books store.

There is a debate about extras in rental units and whether or not the return is worth it. Does a cute bookshelf with good titles on it make a difference? We have to ask ourselves: will it show up in reviews? Will it show up in photos? Will it spark any kind of positive conversation about your rental? If books weren't my hobby, I'd say—yes, you need to have some return on that in your reviews to make it worth it. But since books are my hobby, it seems like *of course, you'd want books in there. Throw a puzzle in too.*

You know you, so lean into that. You might know that you and your friends love gaming and having a gaming system would be attractive to a large group of renters. You may be more into the outdoors and think that people would enjoy bikes or hiking equipment (walking sticks, crampons, etc.). Whatever it is, you will likely have the most success and do your best if your broader interests are reflected in the rental.

States + Cities

This section will focus on where remote workers are leaving and where they are going.

Because of the NPR article referenced at the beginning of this book, we know that people have been leaving New York City and San Francisco. Part of what makes a city a *good* city is restaurants, culture, and people of all stripes. I do not think people will be avoiding cities forever or that it's a comment on the policies of those cities; what I do think is that people are leaving places that are cost prohibitive. And San Francisco and New York are cost prohibitive. For that reason, people who can leave are taking their larger salaries and moving to areas with cheaper housing and better quality of living (That's what has been happening in Colorado for the past ten years, but it's also what has been happening in Austin, Salt Lake City, Portland, Boise, etc.).

Fleeing the Expense

The top ten most expensive US cities to live in according to *Education Loan Finance* are as follows:

10. Boston
9. Queens
8. Arlington
7. Oakland

6. Seattle
5. Washington, DC
4. Brooklyn
3. Honolulu
2. San Francisco
1. Manhattan[xxxvi]

After considering that a few of these locations are metros of larger cities, there are seven extremely expensive US cities: Boston, New York City, Arlington, Seattle, Washington, DC, Honolulu and San Francisco.

According to *Kiplinger*, San Diego, Los Angeles, and some Alaskan cities also make that list.[xxxvii] Since these places can cost anywhere between 25-100% above the national average to live in, it makes sense that people are leaving for a variety of reasons—they want to try something new, want to save money, want to do more with their existing money. Tony Robbins has long asserted that one of the best ways to save money is to move somewhere cheaper.[xxxviii] It seems like people are finally listening to him.

Fleeing the Weather

In Colorado, where the sun is ever present,[xxxix] we get a lot of people who are tired of their weather back home. Places with tunnels between the buildings are always an excellent indicator of absolutely miserable weather. The Midwest has a lot of tunnels connecting buildings. I'm sure this is true of many places, but likely because Colorado is in the center west of the country, I meet the most people coming from the Midwest. Counter to popular opinion, Colorado does not have harsh weather. We get snow in the mountains and spring snow in the cities, but we also get intense sun—which burns off that snow quickly.

Here's a list of places in the United States that have the harshest weather:

1. Minnesota
2. Michigan
3. Alaska
4. North Dakota
5. Maine
6. South Dakota
7. Wisconsin
8. Idaho
9. Montana
10. Massachusetts[xl]

I pulled these two lists (most expensive places and worst weather), so that you can understand what your future tenant (American Nomad) may be escaping. We'll talk later about where the nomad is headed when discussing their motivations.

Personality

Beyond income, age, demographics, and geography, who are these people? This is probably more important than anything else we've covered about the American Nomad because while lots of people will have the opportunity to move and work remotely after COVID-19, not all of them will take advantage of it.

While we know a large portion of digital nomads in the past have been working, retired, or independently wealthy, the focus of the expanding tenant pool and people entering this model are remote workers—which means they work. The reality is, you don't care who they are as long as they rent out your place, but the expanding tenant pool is still working. People who couldn't move before because they were tethered to their jobs are on the move now.

Successful remote workers will be disciplined.[xli] These people took courses online during college, they avoid procrastinating and reflect discipline in all sorts of different ways: adherence to a diet, exercise, spending, etc. To work remotely, and to work from a new city, these people must self-manage and have the ability to meet deadlines without the boss present.

This point is important because if these remote workers are high in discipline with their work, they may also be very clear about what they will pay for your rental and what they expect to get out of it.

I'm about to talk about personality in regard to gender, and I'm afraid it's going to sound sexist the way your totally sober uncle unembarrassedly informs you at Christmas Eve dinner that mansplaining isn't real, and definitely not offensive. In fact, he explains that when men pay attention to you, it's because they think you're cute. This comes just hours after you thanked him for your Christmas gift and he replied, "Glad you like the earrings. I had the front office girl pick them out."

I don't want to do that. I don't want to piss you off or offend you or make you feel like I'm a jerk who doesn't know anything about anything. So, this following section is just based off my experience and only my experience. Please read it knowing that it's anecdotal and not fact.

Ahem.

Females who do remote work and travel tend to be organized, communication-driven individuals (Type-A if you will) and for that reason, cleanliness and inventory may be important to them. They will know if you promised there would be a cutting board and there was not. They will expect the place to have been professionally cleaned before they arrived. Basically, they will pay their bills on time and be model tenants, but they will also have equally-high standards for the landlord (Don't be afraid of this kind of tenant—anyone who has high standards for themselves, and subsequently for you, will push you to do better). Also, they may be open to paying more for a higher-quality product.

On the flip side, male remote workers often have more relaxed standards, and will not be as ideal tenants. What does that mean? They typically won't keep the place as clean, communicate as well, or pay as much. Similar to what we see when we have clients shopping for homes, the men are less concerned by the setup and aesthetic, and more interested in the location, the yard, the garage, and their access to hobbies. A lot of men (especially single men) would prefer to pay less for a space that is not as nice than more for a place with extra touches.

We do see trends in real estate and in rentals sometimes, and it is to your advantage to at least give them some thought. If you think gender is irrelevant to your strategy and not worth further thought, I get it. However, before I was in real estate I was in marketing, and because of that I still spend a ton of time thinking about human differences, preferences, and motivations.

Finally, I'm not saying one tenant gender block is better than another. I'm saying sometimes you see different personality trends across different genders. Who you rent to will likely depend on a few things: the pros and cons of the property you already have, and your motivating factors (money, safety, etc.).

A real-world example of this was when we transitioned our personal residence into an investment. We felt our personal three-bedroom condo would appeal more to females and couples as it had nice furniture, great views, great light, extra security, and a higher price point. It was important to us that it was well taken care of and that we secure a tenant who was willing to pay more. While we currently have two males in the unit, we have previously found that at the extra price point, we usually rent to females or heterosexual couples.

Another real-world example is the rental my husband occupied when we met. It was garden level. It had terrible light. The shower looked like a dorm for STDs. The kitchen barely existed. There were literal bars on the window. However, the location was hard to beat. We knew we needed to advertise it at a lower cost and be transparent: a great place to crash if you want to experience the city and are comfortable living with minimal light in a neighborhood that merits window bars. I personally wouldn't want to stay in a place like that since I've watched enough *Dateline* to know that IT'S ALWAYS THE HUSBAND, but when it's not: it happened on the garden level of an apartment complex. However, some women may have avoided exploitative, murder-based entertainment, realized the likelihood of bad things happening was not very high, and had no issue renting the place. Again, this is just a pattern we see, the way the police always see a pattern: husband/boyfriend/lover.

Their Experience

The final piece to understanding the remote worker, aka, the American Nomad, is what their experience often entails.

We know because we've come this far that the American Nomad is well-educated, high-skill, and has an adventurous spirit. For the ones considering nomadism as a response to the COVID-19 crisis, we assume they spent some of the isolation considering what they didn't like about their lives. In response, they are seeking new destinations and experiences.

This new lifestyle can terminate one of three ways:

1. they move on to their next city or experience

2. they seek out a long-term solution (unfurnished rental or purchase)
3. they return to their roots and move home

Next City of Experience

These people will move to their next city of experience because they want to avoid getting stuck again or because their adventurous spirit compels them to try something new. Some of them will come to your city because their previous life wasn't what they wanted it to be, so they are trying on a few new lives/cities to see what does feel right. For this reason, they intend on being with you for one to three months, and then want to try out the next thing to avoid feeling stuck. Similarly, someone may want to be on the move. They are most comfortable with a new experience and are motivated to keep moving and find that next place. Whether it's that, or the person just doesn't want to get stuck in another situation they aren't happy with, this subgroup will move on quickly: one to three months.

While this subset will be your shortest-stay renters, they still stay long enough to minimize the work you have to do: *ahem*, cleaning. They also pay more than the standard long-term tenant. And, unlike Airbnb and short-term rentals, in 99% of American cities (if not American condo HOAs) they are totally legal.

Seek Out a Long-Term Solution

We find that a lot of tenants fall into this pool, and we love the ones that do. Why? Because they present to you like the first group (adventurers, ready for constant change), they sign your lease at a slightly higher rental price, and then they get complacent. They like the space. They like their relationship with you. They like the location. They have come to think of the furniture as their furniture. They come back to you and ask if they can extend the lease. They extend for another four months. Then another three. It's not uncommon for these people to end up staying for a year, but at the elevated price point. As a landlord, this particular tenant is appealing because they are a long-term tenant paying medium-term rents.

However, all good things must come to an end, and as months pass, these tenants think about the cost of rent and how they could save money. (1) they could find a long-term rental and get their own furniture or (2) they could buy their own property.

Sometimes, people decide to buy in your city after you've rented to them, and it's kind of heart-warming. You were part of an experience that led someone to think they wanted to join your broader community. They tried it out and decided it would improve their lives to live there. It's a great feeling to be involved, however loosely, with that. We are excited whenever our tenants transition into buyers because we love Denver and Colorado Springs. We love it when people share our enthusiasm for a great quality of life.

Return Home

As someone who has worked from home part time since 2012 and full time since 2016, I will attest that the experience can be lonely. When COVID-19 started, I had an idea that remote work would become all the rage and this forced experiment would force Boss Dinos to allow working from home. I was right, but I also forgot about the other piece: loneliness.

I don't always like people, but I do like being around people. People are interesting. Whether or not I agree with what they are doing, or want to engage with them about something, talking to people always gives me something to think about. I might think they are weird. I might think they are charming. I might think they are reprehensible. Regardless, being with people helps me feel connected to other human beings, the world, and the culture around me. And as we all learned in 2020, when you work from home every day, all day, you lose this.

People often report being lonely as a pain point of nomadism. In the past, you could drop out of the lifestyle and return to a job with in-person coworkers. We still don't know the future of in-person, high-skill work. However, we do know a lot of people will eventually quit your rental to return to their tribe.

Before we move into the next section, let's revisit why remote workers matter. They matter because they are a growing tenant pool, they have travel flexibility, many of them have higher salaries, and they make excellent tenants.

Part II | A Guide for Landlords

In this section, we'll address what remote workers want, variations in remote worker demographics, and how to target remote workers with your marketing. Whereas the previous section was about knowing the remote worker, this section will talk about how to cater to remote workers.

Before we start though, I want to point something out. There is no right answer to how your place should be set up. While I believe you can market best to people who match your interests and stage of life, plenty of people have had success learning a different audience and marketing to them.

As someone who helps people getting started with real estate investing, I tell my investors: do what's easiest. This is your first investment, which should be seen as your freshman level 101 real estate course. You need to learn the basics without getting in over your head. For that reason, find places that are basically turnkey ready, at most need a coat of paint and *maybe* carpets ripped up. You don't want to lose time and/or be burdened with finding contractors while worrying that something you did is going to sink your family financially. Acquire an easy property. Learn the ins and outs of advertising the property, collecting rents, furnishing it, etc. You can graduate from there after you have the first one under your belt.

This is true for renting to American Nomads as well. If this is your first go at it, don't overthink it. Do what you know. See if you like it. See what you learn.

.chapter three.
What Your Tenant Will Want

In this chapter, I'll cover some basic high-level features that tenants are going to want across the board and should be considered must-haves for the success of your rental.

The table below shows what renters consider most when looking at a property. Unsurprisingly, location and price are top of the list, followed by safety, appearance, floor plan, and home amenities. These are important factors to consider; some of them can be fixed and some can't, depending on whether you already own the property, or your budget. This chapter is meant to help landlords embrace what tenants want, and ultimately, make your property more attractive to future renters.

Table

1	Location	81%
2	Rent	81%
3	Safe Neighborhood	73%
4	Appearance and Cleanliness	69%
5	Floorplan or Layout	58%
6	Home Amenities	55%
7	Pet-Friendly	54%

8	Quiet Neighborhood	53%
9	Light	34%
10	Community Amenities	31%
11	Aesthetics and Charm	31%
12	Energy Efficiency	30%
13	Property Management Reputation	25%
14	Child Friendly	23%
15	Fun Neighborhood	23%
16	Eco Friendly	17%
17	Services	17%[xlii]

If we pulled a list of top priorities for furnished rentals aimed at remote workers, the must-have list would be very similar. I believe the main difference would have to do with Wi-Fi speed and the existence of a desk. That said, I believe this to be a good reference for amenities tenants care about, and your purchase and marketing should adhere closely to this list.

Location

This book is being written in the first half of 2021. The last twelve months have been a real doozy and the beginning of 2021 was interesting too. I mention this because while location has always been a focus of investments, in 2021 we saw changes in where to focus your investments.

Cities

In the past, renters paid a premium for city living. People wanted access to restaurants, bars, sporting events and other people. For that reason, it was more popular and more expensive to live in coastal areas and larger cities (New York, San Francisco, Chicago, Boston, Seattle, etc.). Now some cities are losing population.

According to a January 2021 *New York Times* article "They Can't Leave the Bay Area Fast Enough," residential rents are down 27%,[xliii] and according to an August 2020 article in the *New York Times*, "The Office Will Never Be the Same," "…searches for homes in rural areas are up 76 percent from last summer and suburban searches grew 63 percent."[xliv] (More on that in a bit.)

I have two theories about city living: (1) secondary cities are where we are seeing the most growth, and (2) cities will come back, so right now is a great time to get a discount on a condo.

Theory 1: Secondary Cities

Per *Wikipedia*,[xlv] city populations rank as follows:

	City	Population change from April 2010 to July 2019
1.	New York City	1.98%
2.	Los Angeles	4.93%
3.	Chicago	-.06%
4.	Houston	10.48%
5.	Phoenix	16.28%
6.	Philadelphia	3.8%
7.	San Antonio	16.56%
8.	San Diego	8.91%
9.	Dallas	12.17%
10.	San Jose	8.02%
11.	Austin	23.85%
12.	Jacksonville	10.92%

13.	Fort Worth	22.72%
14.	Columbus	14.17%
15.	Charlotte	21.09%
16.	San Francisco	9.48%
17.	Indianapolis	6.82%
18.	Seattle	23.83%
19.	Denver	21.17%
20.	Washington	17.29%

The above listed cities are the big ones, the serious cities if you will. They have already been discovered, meaning they are already competitive, full of people, and likely quite expensive.

The next-level city is most interesting to me for emerging trends. I refer to these as *secondary cities*. These aren't necessarily cities 21-40 in population rank so much as they are cities close to those larger, expensive cities and/or smaller cities with no immediate geographic competition. For this list, we include Boise, Colorado Springs, Raleigh, Memphis, Nashville, Milwaukee, Fayetteville, Oklahoma City, Kansas City, etc. These are communities that aren't prohibitively expensive (yet), where you have access to restaurants, culture, nightlife, etc. These secondary cities have a lot of buzz around them and they're where we are seeing popular commercial investments going in (think Topgolf, Orangetheory). Basically, businesses that can only exist if their clientele has disposable income. We want to pay attention to these glamour businesses.

Side note here: my investing philosophy is: don't overthink investing, just pay attention to glamour businesses. I call this my Orangetheory *Theory*. Glamour businesses like Orangetheory have paid professionals to understand where they can franchise. Those paid professionals know more about the demographics of a city than I do. For that reason, I (and you) want to follow where those businesses invest. Anecdote: supposedly Burger King spends no money looking into real estate markets; they just follow McDonald's wherever McDonald's goes. I'm not saying you should follow McDonald's, but what Burger King is to McDonald's, you should be to Topgolf, Orangetheory, Panera, Starbucks, etc., and buy there. *That* is my Orangetheory *Theory*.

Theory 2: Cities Are Coming Back

Cities are coming back.

There are two types of people in the world: those that like nature and those that like cities. For those that like cities, they'll want to be in the thick of things again even when their work no longer demands it. And because work is actually not the reason we like cities. We like cities because we can eat at charming restaurants, people watch at parks, see an independent film downtown, and have easy access to comedians, sporting events, and plays. Even more than that, I believe people miss other people.

A Word About Rural Areas

There's rural and then there's *rural*. My husband is from southwestern Missouri. To me, rural means driving for hours through redundant crops, occasionally interrupted by a gas station or a billboard threatening you with Hell in the afterlife.

It's my opinion that rural investments off the interstate will be a hard sell for younger Americans. To begin with, people still like to get laid. For places with smaller populations, the dating game can prove to be a lot harder, *especially* if you fall outside of that heteronormative category.

Rural America and smaller towns are friendlier for two-income (remote work) families that have kids. If you have a property in this kind of community, I'd think about things that would make renting your home attractive to this type of family, such as a large yard, quiet cul-de-sac, making it animal-friendly, etc.

The rub with this will be Internet. Internet can still be tough to come by in some of these communities, and we know that's hands down the most important amenity (let's call it a utility) for remote workers. If you can get strong Wi-Fi in your rural property, you may have an opportunity to rent it at an elevated price to those who want to live with the decreased economic pressure that rural living can offer. If you can't figure out the Internet piece, it will be hard if not impossible to rent.

Remote Worker Incentive Programs

One more note on this: there are towns and small cities in the United States that recognize the power of attracting younger tech talent, and they are getting competitive about finding them. City governments are offering housing and rent stipends, travel stipends, tax breaks, and cash to move to these areas. Kansas, Iowa, Minnesota, and Georgia are part of the list of states offering incentives.

The new website MakeMyMove.com is a marketplace tracking these offers. Their directory to date has thirty-seven relocation offers. The site makes it easy for a tenant to see what the high-level benefits are depending on the city, and allows the remote worker to submit a customized wish list called "Design Your Own." Some of the examples of wishes listed are: I want a bike, I want a monthly credit for co-working space, I want vouchers for local businesses including restaurants and gyms, etc.

Airbnb is also paying attention to and supporting offers for remote workers. "In a recent survey conducted by Airbnb, over one-third of US consumers expressed interest in staying in an Airbnb listing to 'try out' a new city or neighborhood before moving permanently... Airbnb will offer select Tulsa Remote members a $150 gift card, so that they too can 'try before they buy' their new home in Tulsa."[xlvi] Airbnb is investing money and intellect toward this trend, which means maybe you should too.

While this is great for tenants, landlords should pay attention to these trends as well. If you buy in a city actively recruiting young tech talent, you may very well start to see your tenant pool expand.

I love that these cities are so innovative, *but* it might also suggest these cities are struggling. For that reason, I might pay attention to who has been doing it the longest or has the best perks, track that for six months, and see how it is going before investing in an area like that.

Pet-Friendly

My dog Monday loves eating paper towels, peanut butter, and scrambled eggs. She's not always easy to please and it's completely accurate to say her wish is my command. I will basically do anything to make my little princess happy, and there is absolutely no way we would move across the United States without her. She is my number one non-negotiable and we won't even consider your place if we can't bring our best girl with us.

There are approximately 123 million families in the United States, and an estimated eighty-five million of those families own pets. That's 67% of the US population.[xlvii] Dogs are by far the most popular at sixty-three million families, followed by cats at forty-two million. The pet industry is a seventy-five-billion-dollar industry. 57% of single women have pets and 44% of single men have pets. Single people who own pets consider them family members.

And, yet, despite the massive market, only 3% of Airbnbs allow for pets.[xlviii] This is a HUGE opportunity for you.

There is a limited pool of properties that allow for animals, but the newly freed remote worker interested in exploring the United States may very well have a pet. This is because a lot of upwardly mobile people are not having kids (or not having kids yet) and those animals, like Monday, are their kids.

What are the implications for you? How should you think about it when considering how to be attractive to tenants with pets? Is specific marketing required? Are certain types of properties better than others? How do you protect yourself?

This doesn't need to be an animal hotel because the return on investment for pet upgrades is low. Our only goal with being pet-friendly is to widen our rental pool, which will keep our vacancy rate low and allow us to charge slightly more.

The first and most basic step you can take is to state that you are pet friendly. Put it in the headline if you notice that none of your competition is advertising that point. *Pet-Friendly Two Bedroom Condo Near Downtown* sounds great or *Pet-Friendly One Bedroom Near Popular Bear Creek Dog Park.* Just as people start moving out of the city because they want their kids to play with other kids in the suburbs, pet owners start to include their animals' needs in their plans.

This is not an investing or business strategy, but it is a marketing advantage if you can speak to it. I absolutely would be interested in a place if I knew it was close to a nice dog park because I currently live near a nice dog park, and watching my dog play with her dog friends each afternoon is a highlight of my day. The bottom line for this is simple: (1) allowing animals is enough and doesn't require much else, and (2) advertising this point will give you a competitive edge.

If you want to go above and beyond for your tenants, here are a few extras I'd think about:

Dogs

1. **Crate:** You will be doing yourself and your tenant a favor. A crate with a nice pad in the bottom and a blanket over the top will create a safe space for the dog coming to your house and save your tenant the hassle of lugging an awkward/heavy/large item across the United States. Some people might have to travel with a crate anyway, but for those that don't, it'll be a nice addition.

2. **Dog Bed:** This can be the pad in the crate or something else. I just know my dog uses her beds a lot, and it's why she has (plural) dog beds.

3. **Dog door and fence:** Depending on the cost, I'd consider adding this modification if it is cheap-ish and if you are going after dog owners. I would not add a fence to attract dog owners (since fences are expensive), but I would advertise both of these in a huge way, perhaps even with a dog section: our house comes with a spacious, fully-fenced backyard, a dog door for ease of bathroom access, etc.

4. **Contact info for dog sitting/walking:** If you know someone in the neighborhood who is a great dog sitter or walker, leave this information for your tenant. It'll be a huge help to someone who is busy with work, or decides to do a weekend getaway without their animal.

Cats

1. **Litter box:** having a litter box on site with one fresh bag of litter is appropriate. I wouldn't do more than that. This is hygiene maintenance, and for medium term renters that is their responsibility, not yours.

Fun facts about animals and rentals:

- 75% of renters have pets
- 60% of that 75% have difficulty finding pet-friendly properties
- rental damage broken down between people with and without pets looks like this:
  o average $323 in damage to a property from people without pets
  o average $362 in damage from tenants with pets[xlix]

It costs you more money to rent to people with pets ($39 in this study) but you can charge a $200 pet deposit and/or a $50/month pet rent fee, so you actually come out ahead when you rent to pet owners and widen your pool. Allowing for pets is a smart landlording strategy.

Fees for Pets

We allow people to bring pets because we like the larger tenant pool and have not run into any significant issue with people bringing in pets. That said, it's important to protect yourself, and we recommend doing that by:

- Adding an extra $150 non-refundable pet cleaning fee. This will be a lifesaver if someone brings in a dog breed that sheds a ton.
- Charging a pet deposit, a monthly pet rental fee, or both.
  o The pet deposit allows you to charge a fee up front to help protect your property. The advantage is that you have the money immediately. The disadvantage is that if there's a disagreement over "damage" you may not be able to keep as much of the deposit if the tenant pushes back.
  o The pet rental fee comes in every month and is non-refundable. You could also make the pet deposit non-refundable but that's a trickier conversation. Charging pet rent is something a lot of people seem to understand and accept as a cost for bringing their pet.

Rules for Pets

My biggest concern about renting to dogs is noise and angry neighbors in a condo, and my biggest concern about cats is their vindictive streak and urinating on and/or scratching expensive furniture.

It is worth it to send a specific email addressing these points and having the tenant attest to their animal's behavior. It's just one more stop gap where you are saying: *these could be issues, will you write me back and tell me they are not?* This will stop most people who have pets with these issues from proceeding, which is what you want.

Here is some potentially helpful language:

> *… if dog receives more than two neighbor complaints, lease will be terminated and deposit will be withheld.*
>
> *… tenant agrees furniture was in _____ condition (provide video) and that they will pay for any animal damage, etc.*

As far as cat urine, that is a harder nightmare to protect against, so it's something you may want a big deposit on with a specific line addressing cat urine.

Your Insurance

We'll talk more about insurance in a bit, but my husband has always advised being super transparent with your insurance company about how you are using your property. It's not only the right thing to do, but the smart thing to do. If you are lying to your insurance, they will find out and they won't insure you, which makes having the insurance pointless.

I recommend telling them you are renting out your entire space or part of your space, and also that you are allowing animals. The company can tell you which animals they won't cover—certain dog breeds definitely come up on this list—and then you can find other ways to protect yourself (maybe the tenant carries special insurance for that type of breed) and/or you can decide not to rent to that person.

Parking

Even though American Nomads are not committing to a city or a long-term rental, they have likely committed to a car. Note: they usually only show up with one car, even if they arrive as a couple. If you live in an area where parking is coveted and you have two spaces, it's only necessary to provide these tenants with one space.

Providing one parking space is a must. People don't want to worry about having to search for parking and it will make your place more attractive to have a dedicated space versus street parking. Even if street parking is abundant at your rental, a lot of your tenant pool will be leaving places where the lack of parking is an issue (New York, San Francisco) and it may be hard to convince your tenants otherwise. I'm not saying that if you already own a place without parking no one will rent it. But I am saying that if you are looking to purchase something in the near future with this tenant pool in mind, a parking space should be on your must-have list for whatever property you purchase.

Wi-Fi

Let me be very clear about something: time is money. Also, I'm fairly Type-A, so when I get a call from a tenant about something, I feel an immediate need and obligation to address the issue right then and there. This can feel like a withdrawal from my energy bank. Sometimes that makes me cranky, and sometimes that annoyance leads to a fight with my husband and I'm pissed-off for the rest of the day. Have a tenant call three to four times over the course of two months, and by the fourth call they can hear how annoyed I am. They now feel annoyed, the relationship deteriorates, and they don't renew the lease. Now I've lost a good tenant with totally reasonable expectations because I didn't prepare for them correctly.

To avoid this, I try to set things up right on the front end. Tenants pay money for a good experience, and it behooves you to make it awesome for them. As much as you don't want to be bothered with an issue by your tenants, they also don't want to bother you with that issue. Setting everything up right from the beginning will minimize contact, which will make everyone happiest.

In other words, it is worth it to pay for the expensive Wi-Fi, *especially* for remote workers. To begin with, it's a very common request. And since it's a top concern for the tenants, it should be a top concern for you.

Because you and the tenant may have a conflict of interest (you want to keep the bill low and the tenant wants the best Wi-Fi), the two of you may not align on this. You may think to yourself that you have different ideas of what good Wi-Fi is. You may tell yourself the cheap Wi-Fi is fine/sufficient/something they can manage. And I am telling you: don't do this to yourself and don't do this to your tenant.

Going on the cheap will degrade your relationship with a good tenant over time and that's not good business. Those little annoyances pile up on both sides, and they shouldn't. The tenant pays your mortgage and should be treated with sufficient respect. You can avoid phone calls, distress, and unhappiness if you pay for strong Wi-Fi up front.

International flights have individualized TVs, Wi-Fi, and free booze to distract passengers and keep them passive. People who hate flying are much less prone to getting stuck in their heads and acting crazy on a flight if they are enjoying their fifth straight hour of *Top Chef* (I know because I'm a crazy person who gets stuck in my head on flights: *How is this thing staying in the air? How long would you know you are going to die before you die if it goes down? Is a short death better than a prolonged death?* Suffice to say, I'm thankful for TV on flights). The same theory applies here. Your tenants are going to be subdued as long as they can surf the Internet, play games online, or watch movies and television. Probably the number-one way to get a chill tenant is strong Wi-Fi.

Think of expensive Wi-Fi not as a gift to your tenant, but as a gift to yourself.

Storage + Organization

People have a lot of stuff. Even if the rental you provide them is furnished, which it should be if you are planning on renting to American Nomads, they will arrive with more stuff.

It's advisable to have garage storage, an empty closet, or a crawlspace for their stuff. If you don't have that, you should add storage. This can be as simple as throwing basic shelves up or purchasing very cheap shelving units via Amazon that are easy to put together.

Regarding additional organized spaces, nothing excites me more than The Container Store, and there's nothing I'd rather see than a closet built out to have a place for shoes, unmentionables, an area for shirts, an area for pants, an area for purses, a rack for jewelry, and on, and on ... And I'm not alone. Remember those Type-A female renters that pay rent on time but want two cutting boards in the kitchen, not because they even cook but because two cutting boards in the kitchen was promised?? That's me! That's how I get! And I'm not alone in my OCD and my love of all things organized.

Even people who aren't organized like the idea of being organized. Organization *always* photographs well, even if added bathroom, closet, and office shelving may or may not ultimately be used. No one thinks they will move across the country trying to be a better version of themselves and envisions a messier existence (my husband would argue tidier does not mean better person/self/humanitarian, but I digress). They are going to look at the storage and organization options and think, *"Yes, that's me in the future even if it isn't me now."*

Final note on the organization stuff: like appealing to pet owners, you don't need to overdo it, but I believe it makes a difference. It will photograph well. Those photos will add extra eyes. The extra volume of interest will keep you rented more consistently and at a higher price. All that said, don't go crazy on this and don't spend a ton of money on it. Cheap shelves are known to be camera-friendly.

Office Supplies

I've worked from home at least one day of the week as far back as 2012 and moved to full-time work-from-home status in late 2016. This is important only to say that even in a remote work world, certain office supplies remain popular. While no one is going to rent your place a second time just because you provided staples, your first photos should be office supplies or an organized desk drawer. This signals to potential tenants that business gets done here.

Here's what I recommend for an office set up:

- a desk
- a decent chair
- a second screen (consider elevating on the desk so it doesn't take up too much room, or attached to a wall near the desk)
- three pens
- Post-it Notes
- a notepad (keep these cheap as they'll likely leave with the tenant)
- desk organizer
- white board
- corkboard/push pins
- stapler/staples
- scissors
- directions to the closest FedEx

Here's what I don't suggest offering:

- A printer → While 66% of remote workers print out docs at home,[1] printer ink is expensive and printers often break, so this seems like a definite way to waste money and to spend a lot of time on the phone with your tenant.

It kind of blows my mind because these suggestions are so basic, but people respond to them. They are happy to have them and not have to blow a bunch of money at the grocery store to acquire office basics.

To know your tenant is to make your money. It is not rocket science but putting yourself in the position of the tenant will help guide how you set up your space for the remote worker. Spend a few hours considering this now and make more money for years.

.chapter four.

Landlords: Demographics

Airbnb is full of smart people who follow these trends like it's their job because it is! Let's just go ahead and see what they are reporting.

- Nearly 40% of longer-term stays were booked for one person.
- Nearly 40% of longer-term stays included two people. Survey respondents shared that the additional person in their booking was most often a significant other.
- A little more than 20% of longer-term stays were booked for three or more people, with guests most frequently telling us their trips included a significant other and child[ren].[li]

And
- 60% of longer-term guests were working or studying during their stays.
- 65% of guests working or studying remotely during their stay reported that COVID was a factor in their decision to book a longer-term stay. Most often they reported feeling newfound

freedom to temporarily relocate while not commuting to offices or schools.[lii]

I'll talk about all of this in more detail, but as of May 2021, couples and singles are your main demographic.

Fair Housing

It's important to understand what the protected classes are for fair housing in the United States under federal laws. Your state may have additional fair law classes (Colorado does), but these are the classes the federal government protects:

- Sex
- Race
- Color
- Familial status
- Physical or mental disability
- Religious creed
- National origin

It is legal to think about how to decorate your place to appeal to a niche you are targeting.

It is illegal to discriminate against anyone that shows interest in your place and is qualified to rent it.

Gender

As discussed before, men and women may (are likely to) have different concerns when renting a home. This section is meant to outline some of these differences and how they will impact you as the landlord.

Females

Let's start with females. Single females to be specific. If we're going to entertain stereotypes here, females are assumed to be your better tenants. In some states, insurance companies charge females less for car insurance because they have fewer accidents and DUIs.[liii] AKA, they are more responsible. While I'm not suggesting you charge them more or less than their male counterparts, I am suggesting that they are responsible, quiet, and pay their rent on time... but that is just my limited experience.

Women may sound like your ideal tenants, but just keep in mind that if we think domestic remote work will mirror that of nomadic international work and/or corporate America, women only make up around 35-40% of the pool. That said, numbers of female domestic nomads may be slightly higher than remote digital nomads because traveling within the US may appeal more to a larger pool of people than traveling abroad. So, if you go after this niche, your tenant pool will be smaller. *However*, it seems reasonable that a place which appeals to a female might also appeal to a male (while the opposite may not be true). So basically, there's a much larger overlap in the Venn diagram of what women will rent that men will also rent, but less so in the reverse.

Safety

Safety will continue to be a priority for females.

Brief terrifying tangent on this subject. I had a friend who was stalked by a man for approximately three months. She was a single female who owned, and still owns, a single-family home on the western edge of Denver. Not prone to drama, she started to notice certain items were askew when she would come home: her living room magazine and television remote were in the wrong place or a dinner plate would be out that she had no memory of using. Her car was broken into, but the thief only took her sunglasses and nothing of value. She didn't think much of it until a few days later when she came home to find a red lingerie set laid out on her bed. This was alarming and tipped her off to other things that were amiss around her house. Large male shoe imprints in the mud outside her window; a pair of her shoes in the backyard had the laces cut out; a neighbor reported seeing someone in her garage. One night she woke up and made eye contact with the stalker as he stared through her bedroom window. Two days later, he was sitting on her front lawn at seven a.m. The police were called repeatedly. Over the course of three months, this friend literally lost clumps of hair as the stalking continued. She had security cameras installed on the exterior of her house. She changed the locks. When visiting, I would find miscellaneous steak knives hidden in different drawers, etc.

In the spring of that year, her stalker threw a chair through another woman's sliding glass window while that woman was home. The stalker was, consequently, apprehended. And, thankfully, that's where the story ends.

At the same time this was happening, I lived in a condo building that had cameras everywhere, required a fob to access, and had a twenty-four-hour doorman. It wasn't something that I gave a ton of thought to until the stalker incident. I then recognized the benefits of multiple stop gaps preventing some absolute creep from entering my house and laying a bra and underwear set on my bed for me to find.

Point being, if you own a condo and it has a decent level of security, this is something you might want to advertise to potential renters. Unfortunately, this is a double-edged sword: while it is attractive to have security, merely mentioning security may alarm potential tenants. It's a smart thing and a good thing to keep your renter safe, so it's important to implement security with that goal in mind.

There are a wide range of scenarios which might make women feel vulnerable: taking the garbage out at night, letting maintenance workers in, sleeping with the windows open, walking across a parking lot at night, etc. The more you can think about these scenarios and protecting your female tenants,[liv] the better.

Here are some options to help your female tenants feel safe:

- installing a Ring doorbell with a camera. This allows the tenant to see if someone is outside the door of the property and who they are. If they are not home when someone comes to the door, the Ring will record this, and they can see who visited the place in their absence.

- lighting. A well-lit parking lot. A well-lit front door. A well-lit back door.
- being dog friendly (half of women who own a dog got the dog primarily for safety.)[lv]

I'm not going to go overboard on safety since the likelihood of something happening isn't very high. Nevertheless, it is something I think about when I am in the dark somewhere alone and a few extra precautions make me feel better.

Natural Light

An abundance of natural light is a feature that cannot be quantified in a Zillow estimate of your property or a Rentometer report about what a studio will rent for. It is subjective and there are no criteria to be selected for when running your numbers. It is also something that is very appealing to most tenants, and which you can charge extra for.

Again, because females are the minority gender in the remote workforce, but also your more particular tenant, most things that you do to cater to them will also appeal to men. The difference here though is: *Who will pay more for it? How much more will they pay for it? And how do I advertise this?*

Let's start with the last question first: how do I advertise natural light? Well, first off, you are blatant about it. The headline or one of the first sentences states that the unit has amazing natural light throughout. According to *Homes and Gardens*, the second most cost-effective way to add value to your home when selling it is to add a conservatory or a sunroom.[lvi] I'm not suggesting you do that, but I am suggesting you consider what that is about. Why would someone want a sunroom or a conservatory? It's because they want to sit and eat lunch or read books in good light surrounded by plants. If your place has great light, you should feature this not only with the headline, but also with a photo that demonstrates a cute area where the light is great and you have multiple thriving houseplants (and, yes, for photos, they can be fake).

Your tenants probably won't keep the plants alive, nor will they expect them to be there when they arrive, so you don't need to keep the plants updated or alive beyond the photos. The point is a good photo that demonstrates amazing natural light that will be attractive to most tenants. Plants help make that point.

A final way to advertise this is to ask your outgoing tenants, who you feel will be likely to write a nice review, to mention the great light in the reviews. It's as simple as saying something to them like, "I would appreciate a review. I've found past tenants react well to the natural light. If you liked it, it would help if you could mention something about the light being great." And then if people have questions about the light (assuming they are looking from out-of-state) or want to know why the price is a little higher on your property, you can direct them back to the review. It's obviously much better to have a testimonial from a previous tenant than asking them to just take your word for it.

Who will pay for more light and how much more will they pay? This is anecdotal, but women will pay more for natural light. My theory is that women will (1) reject a dark space, and (2) might pay more for a well-lit space. As for younger men, I feel they will be open to a darker space, be into a well-lit space, but may not be willing to pay for that addition in an otherwise all-things-equal situation.

There is no useful rule for how much more someone will pay for natural light, but we know great light is important. Despite your advertising, the majority of people renting from you will be relying on photos they are seeing without seeing the space in person. It will be harder for them to see the value in natural light aside from pointing them back to the reviews.

Laundry

I know. I know. I'm such a sexist, but again, females will care more about laundry and be more willing to consider it a must-have in their criteria. While in-unit laundry is more attractive, on-site laundry is probably equally sufficient. Basically, if your female renter will be staying for more than a month, I doubt she wants to spend any of that time driving three miles to access a laundromat and sit there with a bunch of strangers while her clothes wash and dry. You know what sounds much better than that? Watching *Survivor* on the couch in your living room, waiting for the timer to go off.

I don't think males will care about this as much. Single males do their laundry a lot less frequently than single females and I also think the experience of doing it in a laundromat surrounded by strangers will be less off-putting to them.

That said, I live in Colorado and it's a desert. I recognize it is a more forgiving habitat for laundering laziness than say, the South, would be.

Aesthetics

Like light, having taste is an intangible that is (1) subjective, and (2) not something that can be captured in a Zillow estimate or selected-for criteria. However, having modern, current furniture or an eye for design will attract more attention to your listing, and subsequently, more money.

One thing to think about with your marketing is that you are competing with other listings. The tenant plugs in a few basic criteria (location, timeline, number of guests) and is shown a page (or pages) of listings. If this isn't totally obvious, the tenant makes their next decision almost entirely on your main listing photograph.

Snap judgements are being made off that first photo, so it is the most important part of your advertisement. The photo should be light (so the tenant isn't required to expend extra mental energy figuring out what is going on). Furniture and objects should be sparse (fewer chances to turn people off with design that is particular to you). And the photos should make sense for the season and the situation.

You can update your Airbnb listing at any time, and you should. Airbnb does not share how its algorithm works, so I can't say this with certainty, but it is strongly suspected that the algorithm rewards updated listings. This is because an update suggests a motivated, invested host that keeps the information current, and the algorithm considers this a stronger result than the listing that has stayed untouched for months.

In addition to receiving algorithm preference, you can avoid the mental and physical disconnect I felt at the prospect of enjoying an outdoor pool in January in ski country (Because of copyright laws, I can't post it here, but I'll say it was the cover photo for an Airbnb in Vail, which I was looking for around the Holidays). That same image includes an outdoor firepit and was clearly located at a hotel. A better photo for a hotel in ski season would include a lobby, a room with a fireplace, or a lodge with a beautiful Christmas tree. An exterior decorated with beautiful white lights. All of these suggest winter and the romance of winter. It's an experience I've already envisioned for myself and it's not hard for me to make the leap or want to know more. Likewise, when summer comes, an appropriate picture for ski country would be beautiful mountain scenery. Since the mountains are still not a place people think of as *hot,* I'd skip the pool photo and concentrate on mountain recreation. This means displaying a picture of hanging mountain bikes or kayaks, outdoor dining, or a stunning view of a mountain range in the distance. Have the main photo reflect the experience the guest expects in seasonally-appropriate ways.

Here's something else: make the first photo unique and DO NOT MAKE IT A PHOTO OF THE BED. Is there anything less exciting than a photo of a bed? What you do in that bed could be exciting, but the bed itself is not. And, anyway, what exactly does that photo tell me? It says nothing about the bed having a comfortable mattress. It basically just says: that person has a quilt I would or would not buy myself; that person does or does not use too many pillows; that bed looks like a bed. Exactly zero information has been imparted to me other than my own personal judgements about your comforter style and your use (or abuse) of pillows. Since people will be confused if they don't see a bed, you should include photos of the bed... but include those photos last.

Remember when I said earlier that organization and shelving goes a long way? Having a photo of an organized home office space and/or desk as your first photo will stand out (especially for a crowd coming to have a work-cation). I can take one look at that photo and know that there will be somewhere comfortable for me to work while I'm there, and also that if I like the style, I'll likely appreciate the style in the rest of the house.

Airbnb has an option for "Dedicated Working Space." You should select this but since people are inclined to define "dedicated working space" different-ly, it would be helpful to show photos of the working space as well as a description of what's available.

Kitchens are another important area and worth highlighting. If you have a beautiful kitchen with a nice island or a breakfast bar, that's a great photo to feature. It will make cooking, hanging out, and working in that space look appealing.

In reviewing a list of fifteen reader favorite photos from *Houzz*,[lvii] six are outdoor spaces (either shot from outside or inside looking out), four are kitchens, two are bedrooms, one living room, one office, one bathroom.

If we think this pattern has significance, then we want to lean into the outdoor experience and the kitchen.

We also know that remote workers are putting a premium on outdoor spaces now that they are planning on spending more time at home and/or because 2020/2021 gave us the pleasure of spending a lot of time at home. Here are a few other items that would maximize outdoor space use and show well in photos:

- a fire pit (just make sure you and your tenants know about local fire and burn laws, what time of year allows for it, and when it's prohibited)
- a couch
- side tables
- an area with shade
- a fenced-in yard for children or a dog to enjoy
- white lights: I can't emphasize these enough. They photograph well, they set a relaxed but festive mood (think any Pinterest board of a wedding you'd like to attend), and they don't cost much.

Males

Television

I had no idea how important a television was until I met my husband and he regularly derided my thirty-inch television. Or maybe it was thirty-two? Point is, I don't know because I don't care that much about the TV. I watch shows, but on a laptop in my bedroom or while I get ready. If it's a live show, I might turn on the TV. Basically, my focus for the television was flatness and cost. Therefore, I got an unacceptably small television.

Lest you think he was being a jerk about my small television, it's backed up by a questionably sexist 1999 Chicago Tribune article that states: "Men buy huge, unsightly TVs." Added to this, our very small television has also shown up in reviews. People have openly mocked the itsy-bitsy TV we provide in a rental against the rather large white wall. It does photograph funny, and last week when we were staying at the place during a break in visitors, I had to admit, "That's a real small TV."

When it comes to avid sports-watching, men out-number women a little more than 3:1.[lviii] My husband has made it clear to me on many a Saturday or Sunday that sports need to be watched in real time, thus it can't be a laptop and must be a TV. Also, HD is a must, and bigger is better.

If you are going after male tenants, this is one thing I'd prioritize. I'd suggest buying something on the bigger side (50+ inches if you can), that is a smart TV (basically the only TVs you can buy anymore). The advantage to the smart television is that your tenants can sign into their own media packages online and watch live sports (YouTube, Hulu, Sling, etc.) without you having to incur the cost of upgraded cable.

Raney | Summit County, CO | Landlord
Colorado Springs (2/2) + Summit County (2/2)

What kind of tenants have you had?

In Colorado Springs, our first tenants were remote workers and they stayed for two months. Our second tenants were building a house. Right now, we have a couple that are remote working and may be moving here. They are renting for one month. After that, we have remote workers coming in from Florida and they are staying for four months.

What about in Summit County?

Because of our access to the mountains and it being more of a remote property, we've had remote workers back-to-back that want the mountain experience.

What have you found your tenants care about?

People want to know about the Internet. They want Wi-Fi that will support Zoom calls all day long. They also want to know where groceries are, but basically, they want to come in, bed down and get to work.

How have the tenants been?

We've had couples and they have been easy tenants.

Where are you sourcing them from?

Airbnb.

How often do you talk to them?

I try to check in with them every ten days. Are you having a great time? Do you need anything? You can kind of read people to see how often they want to be talked to. I text them and say: "No need to respond but if you need anything, let me know."

Have you had to add anything to a property after someone started the rental?

I can dropship Amazon anything. I've offered to do that or let them buy it and Venmo them the money. They prefer to have me do it and have it delivered directly by Amazon.

For one of my properties, they asked if it was okay if we got a desk in here. I said, "Yep. There will be one in two days." It was exactly like the other one. I shipped it through Amazon. I think people like contactless and keeping their anonymity.

I like people and want them to be happy and have a good time. I want them to have what they need.

Any other thoughts?

If you have one review that says your Internet is bad, your bookings will go down.

We tell them we have a high speed, premium package. I send them the speed test, but caveat it by saying if everyone is on the Internet the streaming will be slower, just so they don't feel like they've been lied to.

People don't care about the TV, they care about the Internet. My son-in-law would never let me not get a smart TV. Bigger than I think they need to be. Josh sees it like the Internet and he says don't mess around with it, and I haven't had any complaints.

Doesn't that mean men care about the TV?

Ha! I don't know. He likes finding ways to spend my money!

Dark Furniture

I'm going to go out on a limb and say that twenty-five to thirty-five-year-old men who are renting your space aren't concerned with keeping it clean. And they are definitely not concerned with keeping your space clean after they've had a few drinks and are winding down for the night. For this reason, I recommend having either dark leather or dark upholstery: chairs, couches, comforters, sheets and towels. If you want a rug in the space, make that dark too. One thing to note: dark walls make places look smaller, and I imagine a darker rug does too. Only add a dark rug if you feel it is a must for protecting the carpet and/or preventing anyone from seeing scratches or stains on the floor.

Bar Cart

When you are advertising to men, you need a television, so they know they'll have access to live sports. Absolutely everything else should make them think it would be a nice place to entertain dates. Nothing says this more than a classy bar cart in the living room.

A bar cart immediately invokes the idea of asking someone if they'd like to come in after a nice dinner to have a drink. The bar cart lends a level of sophistication and a nice touch to the end of the night.

For this, we are not keeping the bar cart stocked during their stay, nor are we serving them high end booze. Like almost everything else, what the bar cart needs first and foremost is to photograph well. Better than expensive booze is a sweet little rolling cart (Amazon has cheap options), some nice-looking glasses, and a decanter. The nice-looking glasses can be acquired at Target, as can the decanter, but my experience also suggests that Goodwill and Salvation Army always have an abundance of great glassware and kitchen supplies, so that is where I'd start.

Grill

Post-COVID-19, people have put a premium on outdoor space. To the extent that white lights are cheap and do wonders, a grill does as well. It reminds people of summer, friends, and food. All things worth celebrating.

Couples

The bulk of remote workers will be single men (largest demographic), single women (pickiest but also, possibly, your best tenants), and couples. I believe this because these demographics will have the most lifestyle freedom.

Now that we've covered what a single male and a single female would want from the rental space, let's think about what's different for couples. I'm using the term in an overarching way: could be romantic or friendship, but I'm assuming two tenants and one lease for this section.

Many of the items we covered for singles hold true for couples (aesthetic, a television, laundry, parking, pet-friendly). However, the main way the focus changes for couples is what type of property you rent out. Hint: it's going to need to be bigger.

Couples will likely want a minimum of two rooms, and may want three (we are seeing an uptick in demand for three-bedroom condos currently and believe this has to do with the need for an office now that much of the working population has shifted to working from home, either full or part time post-pandemic).

The Space

For romantic couples, two bedrooms is a minimum because you need a bedroom, and you need an office. Yes, as my husband is fond of pointing out, you could just sit on the couch to do work, but it's nice to have some privacy.

COVID-19 was a great test of everyone's relationships in the entire world. It was a time when you got to see a lot of your spouse. You saw him in your bed first thing in the morning. You bumped into him in the kitchen when you were trying to get coffee. You both looked at each other and then darted your eyes toward the dog leash when the canine whining started. You waited each other out on this point. You ran into each other on the couch while surfing the web/kind of working. *Oh look, he's in the kitchen again while you are in the kitchen, guess we'll be spending lunch together.* You saw him at five when you both agreed to take the dog for a walk. You had an inane conversation at five thirty about what to eat for dinner. You ate dinner together. You watched an hour of television together. You saw him in your bed at bedtime. And repeat.

It's a lot of time together, which is why a second room with a door on it goes a long way to preserving romance.

Unsolicited marriage advice and acquisition of a dog advice: While writing this book, I was nearly lured into purchasing a beagle puppy because beagles are adorable and beagle puppies are unfathomably adorable. My husband was opposed to this because beagles howl and they shed in three different colors: tan, white and brown. "I know. I know," I said, but in a tone that suggested I thought we should probably buy one anyway. He then looked at me and sternly said, "We gotta live with this thing, okay? It can't just be cute." Which I think is also great marriage advice, inside and outside of a pandemic: it can't just be cute. You have to actually like a person, and they have to work with your lifestyle. A beagle puppy is a great idea for a dog park date; it's less of a good idea in a pandemic. The whole point of this paragraph is that I do get sick of seeing my husband all day, every day sometimes, but *man*, am I happy that I actually like him. He's not just a cute beagle puppy, he's smart, easy to live with, and fits my lifestyle.

Wait. Back to the office door. It's useful if you are both working from home and have a professional call or meeting you need to jump on. It is not always convenient to work on the couch if you have agenda items you need to work through with other people on the telephone. Likewise, if you are writing a book about renting a space to remote workers, it's nice to be able to retreat to an office, shut the door, and get into a zone.

If you own a three-bedroom property, consider advertising it as one bedroom and two offices (romantic) or two bedrooms and one office (friends). Alternately, even for couples that only need one office, having a spare room could come in handy if they stay for a while and have friends or family visit. I own a three-bedroom, two bath condo and have rented it out to couples and friends. It is prepared for these people as two bedrooms, one office, but has been converted (by them) during their stays to fit their particular needs.

Children + Families

Let's talk about how priorities shift when you are traveling as a family. If singles care more about what is outside of the unit—proximity to nightlife, other singles, and great outdoor excursions—families care far more about what is inside the unit.

When thinking about what a family wants in a rental, the focus should shift to the ease of living.

For this arrangement, you will want at least two bathrooms and three bedrooms. Two bathrooms is great for resell value, but it's also great for keeping the peace, the privacy, and schedules on track. I cannot overstate how important two bathrooms is. Three bedrooms are important because the kids can have a room, the parents can have a room, and there is additional space for an office.

From my interviews with parents, a well-stocked kitchen is also important. What I mean by a well-stocked kitchen is a kitchen with at least eight drinking glasses and eight knives, eight forks, eight spoons, eight plates, etc. You get the idea. This means mom or dad won't have to wash dishes constantly… BUT, if mom or dad are constantly washing dishes, a dishwasher is very helpful and a much-requested amenity. And finally, for the kitchen, plan to have quality pots and pans, soup pots, spatulas, etc. General cookware items will be important to families (And yes, advertise all of this in your headline if families are the demographic you are going after. *Kitchen comes fully stocked for families: good for cooking at home*).

I think we've all read about how moms are now enjoying *even more work* in this remote world,[lvix] so in addition to a dishwasher, laundry on site will be very attractive to a family staying with you.

Using limited space to create rooms and workspaces is a huge plus for the potential remote work demographic. Some basic ways to make bedrooms function as offices are as follows: Install a floating desk on a wall or take the doors off the closet and put a desk and a chair in one side, while leaving hangers in the other half of the closet.

And finally, adding a fence to your property can go a long way. Many an adventurous family includes young children and/or dogs that need the extra security and protection of a fence.

Heather | Portland, OR | Remote Worker

Finance professional traveling with husband and two sons (10 + 8) and dog, Pepper

What is your background?

In September, we sold our house and started a road trip across the United States.

Who is we?

My husband, two sons (ages ten and eight) and our dog, Pepper.

Are you working?

Yes, I'm a contractor that does finance work for the government.

Where are you now and where have you been?

We are about ten minutes outside of Portland, and we've been to Maine, Vermont, Ohio, Florida, Arizona, and now Oregon. We are going to Washington next, and maybe Alaska after that.

So, what kind of properties have you been staying at or looking for?

We prefer three beds, two baths. However, the price difference between a 2/2 and a 3/2 can be almost a thousand a month, so sometimes we'll stay at a 2/2 to save money.

What do you look for in a property?

A well-stocked kitchen—we've been in places that have four plates, four forks, spatulas, whisks, mixing bowls.

We make bread every two days in the kitchen. I make muffins. We cook dinner every night. The kitchen is really important. We need it to be working.

The beds are important too. New beds, not old, lumpy mattresses you got off craigslist. The rental we were just at, I had to sleep in the kids' bedroom because the master was so uncomfortable. Because of the driving and the beds, my hips and back always hurt. I sound like I'm a hundred years old.

What about working remotely? What has been helpful with that?

Off the top of my head, a desk and outlets, enough extension cords so if it isn't right next to the outlet, I can still plug in.

What else would be useful?

I work off my laptop. If there were a monitor at the house, that would be amazing. I've tried to plug into TVs but it doesn't work well.

If they do have an office set up, it either doesn't show up in the photos or it's even if in the photos, it's not highlighted.

Would you pay more for this?

I probably would pay a little more, like a $100 per month, to have those. Definitely if it's between two equal places, I always pick the one with the desk.

What about your kids? Anything you've noticed on that front which is helpful or unhelpful?

A list of kid-friendly activities would be really helpful.

How much of a discount do you expect to get if you are going to stay for a month or longer?

I usually see about 30% off, but I don't care about that. I put in for a month and look to see if it meets our budget. If it doesn't, then I take it off.

What else?

The last two houses in Eugene and Portland are the only two houses that have had a fully fenced yard. There is always a fence, but there is also usually a gap somewhere with no way to close it. Because of the dog, having a full fence is a huge advantage.

Age

Who is coming to visit? Most likely millennials and Gen Z.

Millennials. You think you know them, but do you? *Wikipedia* reports that you may have heard the term so often it's been rendered a useless buzzword.[lx] I get that since it feels like people love saying "millennial" while throwing around all sorts of wild stereotypes and complaining about our addiction to screens.

Annoying label or not, millennials matter. They matter a lot because they are your remote worker. Here's a few things to know about them: they are turning anywhere between twenty-five and forty years of age in 2021. They aren't that jazzed about getting married or having children.[lxi] They love the Internet, social media, and technology. And, finally, there are seventy-two million millennials in the United States, a generation that is larger than baby boomers.

Gen Z comes immediately after millennials. They are defined as people who were born between the mid-1990s and 2010. According to *Wikipedia*, this cohort likes sexting, good grades, and allergies (meaning they have a lot), and they dislike alcohol, sleep, unplanned pregnancies, and tasks that require having a long attention span.[lxii] They are the first generation to have access to smart devices from birth. What this means for you? Keep the lease short and make sure the Wi-Fi works.

A note on Gen Z and their migratory patterns in 2020. A higher percentage of Gen Z moved during 2020 than millennials. But since Gen Z is between the ages of eleven and twenty-five as of this writing, I think they were moving back into their childhood bedrooms more than moving to new experiences. I'm sure that happened too, and I feel confident that as they get older they will explore more. But I suspect their migration trends during 2020 had more to do with going home to be near mom and dad during a life-changing pandemic than it did exploring.

Education

Remote workers are educated, and that has implications.

Educated tenants will actually read a lease, have a sense of their legal rights, and opinions on what is fair or not fair. They know how to research. And since they know how to research, they will have a sense of what market rates are competitive. In general, it's good business to be a good person. However, if you're an awful person and you don't care about ethics, just know educated people will be more alert to getting scammed.

Income

Whoever had the idea for Tulsa Remote deserves a pat on the back, a raise, and many, many accolades. Whoever you are, wherever you are, *bravo*.

Tulsa Remote was launched in late 2018. The purpose of this program was to bring out-of-state talent into Tulsa with incentives (a $10,000 grant, one year membership in a co-working space, social activities, and help acquiring housing). The hope is that the city of Tulsa will reap long-term rewards from this program. Per the website: "We believe once people come to our growing city, they will want to stay longer than the first year." Frankly, I love the confidence in this statement. Any city worth its while should be able to say as much, and it's very cool that Tulsa put themselves out there. *Yeehaw, Oklahoma!*

This program was one of the first, if not *the* first, to succeed at doing this in the United States, and was so successful (thanks in part to COVID-19), that a slew of other cities are getting in on the game with their own programs. Some of the states offering incentives were New York, Hawaii, Kansas, Mississippi, etc. And yes, while those four states don't share much in common, what they all need is an influx of capital, brains, and remote work to thrive. If you want to see a list of states and their offers and/or customize what you want and submit a package, you can do that at the previously mentioned MakeMyMove marketplace and website, as well as Airbnb at their "Try Before You Buy" page.

I mention Tulsa Remote because[lxiii] they have had an influx of over 1000 remote workers with an average salary of $105,000, and the city has benefited from a major infusion of cash and spending power! According to CNBC, Tulsa Remote succeeded in keeping 90% of their participants beyond the twelve-month program.[lxiv] Brilliant.

Nailing down how much remote workers make can be tough. *FlexJobs* reports that approximately 26% of remote workers make more than $100,000 (and are twice as likely as their onsite peers to make $100,000 or more).[lxv] However, a 2019 CNBC article about people who work from home reports that the median salary is $42,000.[lxvi] Both studies state that across the board, people who work from home full time make more than their in-house counterparts.

I've said this before, but I'll say it again: for your first rental, go with what you know. If you yourself make $40,000 to $60,000, you likely know what the expectation is for that price point in your community. In Denver, $60,000 is going to help you pay for a studio or a place that requires a roommate (the average is $1894 for a two bedroom in Denver),[lxvii] but in Tulsa, you can pay the rent on a two-bedroom apartment (the average is $845).[lxviii] You know your market and you likely have an idea of what you like and what you can do at your price point. Likewise, people who make $100,000+ may have different expectations, but that only goes so far depending on what market you are in. This is beyond obvious, but $100,000 doesn't go as far in Seattle as it does in Cleveland.

.chapter five.

Geographies

Where are they going?

Before the pandemic, 7% of the US workforce worked remotely. In the middle of the pandemic, the remote workforce was between 33-50%. After the pandemic, I assume tech companies and high-skill work may pivot while workforces that require more face-to-face interaction will return to the office. Without knowing how this will play out quite yet, I'm settling on a figure solidly between pre-pandemic and raging pandemic, which gets us to a percentage of remote workforce in the high teens, mid-twenties (think, 18-25%).

Here's where these stats tie in: Prior to the COVID-19 pandemic, the number one state remote workers relocated to was Colorado[lxix] (followed by Vermont and Oregon, Montana and New Hampshire). More people who can move means more people will move, which means cities and places attractive to remote work stand to gain a lot of new faces. Case in point, as I finalized editing this book, Colorado gained its first congressional district in twenty years.[lxx]

Places that were attractive to remote workers before the pandemic will remain attractive during and after the post-COVID-19 era. A lot of the literature on the pandemic suggests people are moving to places for quality of life. While the pandemic can and has done many depressing things, it can't change the weather, the geographic appeal of the mountains, the ocean, or a cute New England town.

Or maybe it can. As outlined in a November 2020 NPR article, "The number of people who moved to Burlington in the spring from bigger cities was double what it was during the same period last year, according to the national real estate brokerage Redfin."[lxxi] The same article cites that these smallish cities also saw a significant uptick in population:

- Santa Maria/Santa Barbara, CA
- Louisville, KY
- Buffalo, NY
- Little Rock, AR
- Tulsa, OK (Tulsa Remote! Someone give that employee a raise!)
- Greenville, SC
- Knoxville, TN
- Syracuse, NY

It does seem like a huge influx of people into these small cities might ruin the charm that attracted people to them in the first place. For that reason, it will be interesting to see how these cities adjust and if the overall long-term impact is positive or negative.

Rural or City?

A common question for me since I started tracking and blogging about remote work is: *What about rural places? I keep hearing people are leaving cities, so should I be buying in rural destinations?*

Again, I don't think we have enough data to speak to this yet, but there are two ways of thinking about this: (1) *Tony Robbins + His Thoughts*, and (2) *No, duh, no.*

Let's start with Tony Robbins!

Tony Robbins: the case for rural

I would solidly be in the *No, duh, no* camp except for the popularity of the FIRE movement (Financial Independence, Retire Early) and the psycho millennials out there making their own nut butters, bragging about wearing the same tennis shoes since high school, and boring everyone to death with their philosophies on minimalism. Not only are these the people you would absolutely hate to sit next to at a dinner party or be married to, but they might also move to rural Wyoming just to finally get that PhD in pretension.

You may be thinking at this moment: "Great, you have a lot of hate in your heart for the FIRE movement, but what does that have to do with Tony Robbins?"

Remember this previously-mentioned 2015 *Business Insider* article by Tony Robbins[lxxii] where he proposes that people who want to get a grip on their finances should consider moving to a cheaper city to make that happen? He's like the original FIRE troll ruining everything fun in life with his devotion to saving money through sacrifice. Just the very pitch of that sentence makes my ears bleed. Ughh, I do not like it.

However, I do think there is a strain of younger people who are not just annoying because they wear old sneakers, but who are amazingly good with money. Case in point, we have some new clients who stumbled across a Facebook post at the start of COVID-19 that said, "Rather than watch *Tiger King*, why not watch the Dave Ramsey series on money management and change your life?" And they actually did just that! They may have still watched *Tiger King*, but they also watched the Dave Ramsey series in early April, and by the time we met them in late October they had paid off $80K in debt, acquired a home, and were meeting with us to acquire another home. Also, they were charming. You would totally want to sit next to them at a dinner party.

I tease the FIRE crowd, but I recognize they are better than the rest of us and will be sitting pretty at retirement. I just question sacrificing your best, healthiest years in exchange for the idea of a robust and satisfying retirement in which you're spending money comfortably and traveling all of a sudden. I don't see that happening, and thus, I have trouble squaring those two things.

The counter to that argument, which I also believe, is that we don't need or enjoy most things we consume. As I type this, I'm lying in a day bed that used to have three blankets but is now down to two because one of the blankets shed. There are at least four pillows on this baby and I'm looking at a West Elm candle that is now just a ceramic pineapple because the wick broke. There are definitely ways to cut back.

There is a strong argument for being frugal, but sometimes I roll my eyes at people who cut out Netflix, drinking, pet ownership, etc. so they can count their Benjamins. My opinion is that money is important, but only up to a certain point.

We purchased our second condo from a guy who had painted the walls off white with a hint of urine, covered every single window with curtains (hiding three quarter windows with views of downtown Denver) and played video games all day. You may be thinking I'm judgmental, but just know that (1) I am; and (2) at closing he announced to his realtor (a woman), our lender (a woman), his buyer (me, a woman), and my husband, that he "does intimidate women because he's too smart for them." Aside from the inaccuracy of his statement, I'm pointing out his fondness for paint colors that resemble sterile human waste and his video game habit to illustrate that the guy could also live in a rural, not-fun place with no issue. If you're going to paint a gorgeous condo in downtown Denver need-more-water-pee color, put up curtains everywhere, and play video games all day, there is zero reason not to move to a less appealing state so you can pay lower rent.

No, duh, no: the case for cities

People like cities. That's why a lot of them live there. They like good restaurants, independent films, diverse people, clothing boutiques/salons/tattoo shops that are abreast of trends. People can dislike other people and still like cities. Cities offer an anonymity that can be hard to find in small towns and people-watching can provide a stimulation that is often comforting.

See Part Two, Chapter Three: *Cities Are Coming Back.* I genuinely believe this, and I do not believe this trend of abandonment for the suburbs will persist or is even real. The reason I believe that is because Denver rental applications were up 11% in 2020 over 2019, and I don't think that was true of Fort Morgan, Pueblo, or Monument (huh? Is Fort Morgan a town in Colorado? Exactly. You've never heard of that city because unlike Denver, it's not coming up in every list of Top 5 Best Places to Live). If you can get a house in Denver at this point, count yourself blessed because you probably beat out a ton of competition. Competitive real estate is also the current norm for city metros/suburbs, but less true for rural areas.

I know people will point to San Francisco and New York, both of which are suffering from city flight, have depressed rental rates, and have not fared well in COVID-19. That is all true, *but* two things:

1. San Francisco and New York's worst real estate market days are a gazillion times better than Tulsa's best real estate day (sorry, Tulsa, you know you have my respect, but truth is truth).

2. Most cities in the United States are not New York or San Francisco. There are a lot of other big and thriving cities that are still expensive and still attractive even if they are not the upper echelon

of international cities. Here are a few just to jog your memory: Denver, Minneapolis, Chicago, Seattle, Phoenix, Houston, Dallas, Santa Fe, Boise, Philadelphia, San Antonio, Austin, Milwaukee, Portland, Memphis, Nashville, and on, and on, and on…

Zillow and Yelp

Because Zillow and Yelp are also interested in this topic, let's briefly touch on what they report. Per a second quarter study they put together in 2021, this movement is just beginning. Because of that and because one is very much a real estate business and the other is very much a consumer trends business, they put together a list of the top ten markets they think remote workers will want to live for one to six months. Stripping out the top thirty largest metro areas, they returned this list based on affordability, housing availability, activities, furniture rental, and vacation rentals amongst a few other criteria.[lxxiii]

1.	Jacksonville, FL
2.	Austin, TX
3.	Boise, ID
4.	Nashville, TN
5.	Charleston, SC
6.	San Jose, CA
7.	Fort Collins, CO
8.	Asheville, NC
9.	Las Vegas, NV
10.	Salt Lake City, UT

.chapter six.

The Property

So, what should you buy? What I'm about to describe is a wish list for the perfect property. This advice is for someone who has not yet purchased and is looking for the best way to support this model. If you already own a property but still want to implement the model, you can likely have success with what you already own. My sincerest hope is that you try out this model because I believe it's (1) quite easy, and (2) the future.

Please don't get discouraged if you read anything below and think to yourself that the property you own doesn't meet the criteria. It doesn't matter. Like a lot of successful ventures in life, much of investing is just showing up. It's making the decision to buy and holding your crippling fear at bay. It's striving for perfection that prevents goal attainment. So, let me reiterate, your property is probably great and will totally work. The property I'm about to describe is a best-case scenario.

Condo v. Single-Family Home v. Multi Family

Property Types

Different property types are popular for different models. Let's discuss.

A Note First About HOAs

Let me talk about HOAs here just so that you can concentrate on everything else I'm about to say without feeling anxious about HOAs. If you've read investment books or spent a significant amount of time on the website Bigger Pockets, you probably think of HOAs as bad and expensive and not part of a serious investment. I strongly disagree with all of that.

Much like everything else in the entire world, HOAs are not a static, one-size-fits-all situation, and it's to your disadvantage to approach them this way. Yes, you should avoid HOAs with high fees, you should avoid HOAs that are imbalanced and no longer allow for rentals (non-warrantable) and you should probably avoid HOAs that don't do very much and have bad finances.

Assuming you can find an HOA that has a reasonable monthly fee and has been staying on top of their major projects and costs. This is reflected in their monthly statements. Good HOAs are HOAS that spend down their reserves every five to ten years on major projects. HOAs that follow this pattern are your friend, not your foe.

I'm a lazy investor: I don't want to talk to my tenants that much. I'm happy if they are happy and I structure almost everything I do around never speaking to them outside of "liking" the Venmo payment they send me every month. Aside from proper maintenance and a strong Internet connection, this can also be achieved with a strong HOA. The HOA takes care of mail, common spaces, community laundry upgrades, the busted garage door, etc. A good HOA handles many issues, and they pay for them as well (albeit through you). For that reason, I love my HOAs and 100% give it up to the people who volunteer their time to make the building I invest in better.

The only criticism I will offer about HOAs is that they can be like having fifty business partners, and that can be frustrating and slow. Because *I guess* I'm kind of controlling, I try to not pay too much attention to the monthly activities of my HOA. I know I probably wouldn't agree with a lot of the board's decisions and since I don't want to be on the HOA board, the best thing for me to do is to be hands-off on that.

Condos + Townhomes

I'm assuming you are interested in renting to remote workers because you are reading this book, and if that is your intention: **the best type of property for a remote worker is a condo or a townhome.**

Our remote work investments are mostly in condos. That is because a condo was the first thing we could afford when we were looking, and because it was also the second thing we could afford. We purchased condos to rent on Airbnb before Denver passed a law in 2017 limiting Airbnb investments to primary residences, and thus, had to pivot because the laws changed. We pivoted at that time to furnished 30+ day rentals (remote workers) and have been very happy with that decision since.

Let's revisit who the remote worker most likely is:

- single or part of a couple
- more likely to be a male
- likely to be under forty

Let's revisit where we think you should buy:

- somewhere that has a diverse economy.

Which places have diverse economies? Cities. Where are condos and townhomes? Cities. Where should you buy? Cities.

Single-Family Homes

If you absolutely cannot get comfortable buying a condo, a single-family home is also a good option, albeit with different strengths and weaknesses.

The advantage to the single-family home is that you have more freedom. This assumes you are not buying a house in a neighborhood with covenants (fancy word for HOA) and thus do not have the extra layer of scrutiny when deciding what to do with your investment. The restrictions you will account for with your investment will look like this: federal laws, state laws, city laws,

HOA rules and regulations. With every rung you descend, you assume a new layer of regulation. So, buying a single-family home outside of an HOA removes another layer of regulation. Aside from that, you also are not tethered to the bureaucracy of fifty votes or whatever your HOA may require to make decisions. As sole owner of the investment and/or one of a few owners of the single-family home, you have more flexibility to do as you want.

The downsides of owning a house (versus a condo) are the increased responsibility and the yard. If there are any issues with the house, they are now yours (or a property manager's) to handle. This includes internal and external issues, and can look like broken appliances, loud neighbors, freezing pipes, snow clearance, roof replacement, etc.

The biggest downside to owning a house to me is the exterior/yard. Shoveling snow off a driveway and sidewalk has to be someone's responsibility and it's either going to be yours or your tenant's. Same for watering the yard and raking the leaves. Even though COVID-19 taught me that I absolutely love yardwork, investors should see large yards as a negative. Xeriscaping is expensive and only works so well. Lawn maintenance is expensive. Grass costs a lot of money and can be hard to grow/require a significant amount of water.

Multiplex

My biggest issue with multiplexes is that sometimes new investors think this is the only option and buying anything else is either antithetical to scaling or beneath them.

The advantage to a multiplex is they are cheaper than buying multiple single-family homes, and you can limit costs by sourcing one professional to address a problem (electrical) in two units at the same location. *But* how often do you need and/or is it feasible to have the plumber come see inside two units on the same day at the same time?

Also, in the current real estate market, duplexes, triplexes, etc. in cities are often out of reach for new investors. Multi-families attract out-of-state money, seasoned investors, and cash. It is difficult for first-time investors to acquire these properties (in Colorado, at least) and it's to their disadvantage to be fixated on such when a single-family house *or a condo* would do well with a remote worker/medium-term tenant instead.

.chapter seven.

Configuration for an Investment

We've discussed location and property type. Let's talk about configuration. The mix of bedrooms and bathrooms will depend on who your target market is and how much money you have. Again, this is more of a wish list than a must have.

Bedrooms

Now that we know my investment theory on condos, single-family homes, and multiplexes, let's discuss how much room you need.

For this type of investment, I would look for a studio or one-to-three bedrooms. Again, this mostly has to do with the population that will be renting the space: singles and couples, likely childless. Those people don't need a ton of room, nor do they want to pay extra for a bunch of room. As one of these people myself, and as someone who has been a landlord to these people, they are much more likely to shop for a property that is smaller and pay extra for its location or aesthetics.

While I believe that studios and one-bedrooms likely return the best numbers for a remote worker investment, I also mention two and three bedrooms so that your remote worker can have dedicated office space or room for visiting friends and family.

I recognize that's neither super helpful or super specific, there may not be a right answer here beyond the amount of money you have to spend. If you only have the money for a studio or single, buy that and advertise that. If you have the money for a two or three bedroom, can see there is local market demand for that and will get a higher rate of return on the larger unit, purchase that.

Bathrooms

In real estate, I always advocate two bathrooms. Two bathrooms make resell much more attractive, it'll save your marriage, and it'll lend some much-needed privacy.

When running my comps in real estate, I care more about square footage and bathrooms than I do about bedrooms. The reason for this is that a bathroom is far harder to add because of the plumbing component, whereas adding a room often just requires drywall and hanging a door.

Privacy

This is more about noise than anything else. Your tenants are working remotely, so whether they arrive single or as part of a couple or family, they are going to need private, quiet spaces with minimal interruption.

To create privacy and to block noise, here are "10 Tips for Soundproofing Your Home Office" from Bob Vila. I am only listing the five that are cheap-ish and easy:

1. solid door
2. door sweep
3. rugs
4. wall hanging (this sounds to me like it has potential to be ugly, so maybe just have the option to do this – I'm thinking something tenants can put up and take down as needed)
5. white noise machine: alternately, the tenant could just use their cell phone for this. That said, telling them ahead of time to download a good white noise app on their phone might cause some alarm bells to go off, so it might be smarter to just purchase a white noise machine and put it on the desk.[lxxiv]

Yards + Outdoor Spaces

Tenants want and covet outdoor space, so having some outdoor feature will make your property more attractive. That said, as much as tenants may want it, outdoor space adds expense and time management for the landlord. For this reason, I strongly recommend a condo with a balcony over yard maintenance. If you are adamant about getting a single-family home, I'd opt for one with a small yard, or xeriscaping most of it (although, again, xeriscaping requires some money and maintenance).

A note here: if you are going to have a yard, add a fence and allow for animals. As we've discussed, there is a paucity of places that are pet friendly. This is an opportunity, and it's a fee you can pass on to the tenant that will help offset or exceed the cost of that yard.

Laura + Carter | Leadville, CO | Remote Workers

Small business owner + corporate professional, one son (16 months) and 2 dogs

Has it been hard or easy to find properties?

Laura: It's been hard to find places with a reasonable nightly rate. Finding a two or three-bedroom has been hard. We are lucky with this one because it has a Nest, a lock on the door, and mattresses—but it is dated and looks very grandma. It worked out for us because we got it on the off season when it was priced more reasonably.

What is the set up?

Laura: We are in a 3/1. Upstairs, two bedroom and one bathroom. The downstairs has the remaining bedroom.

What have you been paying on this?

Laura: $5306.61 for the total. $126/night.

What sort of must haves did you need?

Carter: For sure, high-speed Internet and pet friendly. Our pet friendly need eliminated a lot of places.

Laura: It was really nice to have a full kitchen. Our ideal was a three-bedroom, so Luca could have a bedroom, we could have a bedroom, and Carter could have an office.

Tell me more about the pet-friendly side.

Carter: Yes, the pet thing really limited where we could rent.

Laura: I read *Optimize Your BnB*[lxxv] and they said, allow for pets and events. People think it will end up being a rager if they allow for events, but according to the book, usually it is just commercial events and not a big deal.

Were you charged extra for the dogs?
Carter: There was no extra charge for it here.

Laura: I think they said on the listing it was $30/pet but it wasn't reflected anywhere in the price.

Does the space have a dedicated desk?
Carter: It does. We almost brought our own desk, but we were already like a circus with the dogs, the frogs, and our kid. This is a plain old desk with a regular chair. Nothing exciting.

The only accommodations they made for this was high-speed Internet, landline, and a ton of surge protectors.

How often are you talking to the landlord?
Laura: Once every two weeks; there's only one property management company in town. Crew comes every two weeks and takes trash, etc. to dumpster. They want things to look nice since it is a reflection on them.

We spoke to her a little more in the beginning when we were trying to figure out things.

Are you paying for anything (utilities, etc.) besides just the core rental?
Laura: No.

How do you feel about the different rental sites?

Laura: Compared to Airbnb, Furnished Finder has been a cluster f***. Once we found out that we weren't going to get in the house until August, we had to go back to the drawing board and find a new rental for a few months. Looked at Airbnb, VRBO and Furnished Finder. Lowest was $2200 and went up from there for a two bedroom. Airbnb was out. VRBO was out. I reached out to three people on Furnished Finder and only got one response back.

This woman named Janice, who was crazy, wanted me to fill out stuff on this extra website and kept talking to us like we knew what she was talking about. Then she made me pay through PayPal, which made me super nervous. Like, am I even going to get a rental?

The system for [finding] a long-term furnished rental could definitely be better. It would be way better if there was something that was more friendly or streamlined.

We have paid the deposit and first month's rent.

Are you enjoying yourself?

We are here for the hiking. It has been just a vacation for the mind, body and soul. We just hike and it's been incredible. It's really sweet: there are kids just running around. Our yard is an extension of our neighborhood. It's got a nice hometown feel versus the more touristy areas.

Anything else I should have asked about?

Laura: My landlord is very good at systems. There are checklists for everything. They have Velcro for the remotes. She put a lot of thought into this rental and it's been a pleasure to be here.

Carter: I think it's been a really nice thing to spend six weeks up here. [I was] talking to some co-workers who are doing same thing and they are doing it in Florida.

Laura: Especially if you can rent out your own place at the same time, it feels like a house swap.

.chapter eight.
House Hacking

Maybe you also recognize that remote workers present an exciting opportunity for landlords and want to enter the market, but don't have the money for a down payment on an investment. That's okay. Your primary residence can be your rental. This model is called "house hacking."

House hacking is a technique people employ to reduce their mortgage by renting out extra space in their primary residence. Most cities allow you to Airbnb (short-term rent) or long-term rent portions of your primary residence, and often the entirety of your primary residence, for a set number of days.

I mention this because when thinking about investing strategy, Airbnb-ing your property (short-term) while self-managing it will usually yield the most money. People typically quit doing short-term rentals for two reasons: (1) they are burned out from the demand of frequent cleaning and communication, and/or (2) the regulation for Airbnb has changed in their city. When people stop doing Airbnb for either of those reasons, it is often appealing to move into the medium-term rental strategy, which is a 30+ day furnished rental. This is the rental strategy that most remote workers will want, and while it yields less than Airbnb, it generates a lot more cash than a long-term rental strategy, and the shortened leases allow you more flexibility with your stays.

There are three fairly standard ways to house hack: bedrooms, basements, or ADUs.

Bedrooms

While renting out a bedroom is the least appealing option (both for you as the landlord and the remote worker as the tenant), it is likely the option available to the most people. In this scenario, you convert your second or third bedroom into a space that a remote worker could use.

I don't love this option. A lot of remote workers are in tech, thus they have money to spare, and will probably want an entire space to themselves. Running into the landlord in the yard or the driveway is one thing. Running into the landlord nonstop in the kitchen or the bathroom is called having a roommate and will be less appealing to all parties.

Aside from me being particular about who I want to see and when, this option creates more opportunities for friction: are we going to agree on noise, cleanliness, and Wi-Fi usage? While this will be the least appealing and least lucrative option for house hacking, if you think you wouldn't mind having a roommate because it means cutting down your mortgage significantly, this is a very good option. And again, while the pool of remote worker tenants will be smaller in this scenario, this population is as diverse as the larger high-skill population. Some of your remote workers will consider cost-effectiveness their number one priority and opt to take a room.

Basements

Basements are a great option for house hacking. I like basements for this because they are often un-derused/never used, and you can sometimes access them from an exterior door that makes the space fairly private.

Frequently, the back door of a house will open into a small interior space and a stairway leading to a basement. If you are house hunting, this is what you want to see.

Plumbing in the basement is also important. The basement space must have its own bathroom with the ability to shower. The second thing you want to see in a perfect world is an open space below the upstairs kitchen. Sometimes, you'll find the laundry in this space and/or a laundry sink. If you see that, congratulations, the plumbing you need for a basement kitchen is there. If you don't have a laundry sink, but the space below the kitchen is open and easy to access, it would be smart to ask a general contractor to come over and see what it would cost to pull the plumbing down and install a kitchen in the basement (plumbing, often, can also be tapped from near the bathroom, on the other side of the wall). If this is inexpensive to do, it is worth adding this feature to your basement. If it is expensive or laborious, you can work around it for short-term rentals, but the remote renter staying for 30+ days is not going to wash dishes in the bathroom sink or go out to eat every night (whereas the Airbnb renter may tolerate this better). You could find a remote tenant that would be willing to do this, but they will also pay less.

Laundry is usually in the basement. This issue will need to be addressed before any rental agreement is solidified. Many of my clients arrange to use the basement laundry once a week at a certain time. It's not a perfect situation, however a lot of people are willing to share if it means reducing their mortgage significantly, paying less than a hotel, or being forced to lug their laundry across town to a laundromat. That said, if you can't agree on the arrangement, you (or your tenant) could use the laundromat.

Finally, since we know noise and privacy will be a factor for many remote workers, it is worth installing soundproofing between the floors, and/or using area rugs. Houses that have carpet on the upper floor are far quieter, so if this already exists, you may not need to worry about it.

ADUs

The term ADU stands for "Accessory Dwelling Unit" and is also called a "mother-in-law suite." They are usually a secondary structure on the same lot, or attached to the original home. They can function independently of the main house. They have their own entrance, kitchen, and bathroom. They also adhere to the local zoning, lot size, and setbacks required by the city.

While ADUs are an excellent option, they are often expensive to build ($250,000 and up in Colorado), and gaining city approval and finding laborers can take time. While many people feel enthusiasm for them, we find the money and time constraints are frequently a limiting factor that works against the larger goal of investing.

Sarah | Denver, CO | Landlord

2 Medium-Term Rentals:
- *2 bed/2 bath condo near downtown Denver*
- *1 bed/1 bath basement in her primary*

How long have you been doing 30+ day furnished rentals?

We have been doing medium-term rentals for two and a half years. We started because we were worried about the residency rules, and also because we were having difficulty with a reliable cleaning service, which made the constant turnover hard sometimes.

What do you feel remote workers care about?

We've upgraded the Internet because everyone wanted to work remotely. I've also noticed that closet space and storage space is more important to the remote worker than it was to the short-term renter.

I do feel like the service and experience for a medium-term tenant is more important than it would be for a long-term tenant. What I mean is, a tenant that is there for a year will be less bothered if the AC or the Internet goes out for a week, but if they are there for just a month, it's a bigger deal.

Have you noticed a difference in interest since the pandemic started?

Since the pandemic, we've been getting a lot of thirty day and forty-five day rentals. There is more interest in our 2/2 near the city. Remote workers are making two beds and two baths more marketable. It's either friends or couples; they like the extra room. They seem to be jumping around and doing shorter stints.

What are you making?

On our two bed, two bath condo, we are getting $2700/month after Airbnb takes their costs. On our one bed, one bath (with kitchen), in the basement of our primary home, we are making $1600 per month. The basement unit is not in as hot of a location and appeals more to traveling nurses and people wanting to move to Denver. They have extended their stays more and are okay with a less appealing location.

Advantages to renting to remote workers?

If you get a difficult tenant, they are there for forty-five days versus a year. Someone else told me that they felt their maintenance and damage costs were lower with a short or medium-term renter because they took better care of the place. She thought they were better tenants. I wonder if it's because you see the property more often.

The other thing we like is that my husband's parents can use the place when they come to visit. It requires planning, but we have managed to make it usable for family and friends, which is not something you can do with a year-long lease.

How is your vacancy rate?

For the most part, we have had someone moving in the same day [someone moves out] or the next day.

.chapter nine.
Finding Remote Workers

We'll start to see new marketplaces emerge with the rise of the remote-worker movement and we'll see the existing marketplaces catering to this population. For instance, in 2016, Airbnb recognized that they had a gap in rentals that served disabled people, so they acquired Accomable, a similar, far smaller site that addressed the needs of travelers with disabilities.

During the writing of this book, Airbnb launched the "Try Before You Buy" portion of their website, targeting people who want to live 30+ days in an area before they buy there. This is likely a response to multiple factors: (1) the intensely competitive national housing market is creating a timing issue for sellers who have to sell before they buy, which is causing overlap issues; (2) remote workers who want to visit a city first before finalizing their decision; (3) it's a nice transition for rental owners burning out on Airbnb or living in cities where the laws change. For all of these instances, it makes sense that Airbnb wants to cater to this demographic, and likewise, you should want to as well.

Airbnb is important and we're about to discuss its importance, but we'll also talk about two other tools we've been using: Furnished Finder and Facebook Marketplace.

Airbnb

In 2021, Airbnb is predicted to have 44.5 million users in the United States, and 45.6 million users in 2022.[lxxvi] While this breakdown does not distinguish who is hosting and who is staying, it doesn't matter. We can read that stat and conclude *that is a lot of people.* It's more people than any other platform and will continue to dominate the market. Currently, Airbnb's stock is valued at $100 billion and is worth more than Marriott and Hilton combined.[lxxvii] I mention that because for the foreseeable future, Airbnb will be a major tool for attracting tenants, and with a stock value like that, Airbnb isn't going anywhere any time soon.

Many of my clients like using Airbnb for the medium-term rental model once they realize it's possible. Because we've been told repeatedly that Airbnb is a site for vacation and short stays, it doesn't immediately register to people that the stay length can be 30+ days. Not until very recently (Spring of 2021) was the functionality for 30+ day furnished rentals on Airbnb obvious. The "Try Before You Buy" page now addresses this need.

Airbnb is also getting hip to the new 30+ day furnished rental trend. While "Try Before You Buy" and the new-ish filter for "dedicated workspace" exist, more filters for remote-workers launched in the summer of 2021. These included options to allow remote workers to search by experience or climate preference, with full flexibility on dates, length, and location.[lxxviii] That's not a search people necessarily needed before, as trips in the past were more likely planned around set vacation days, family and friends, or an area they knew. Airbnb is banking on the fact that workers are flexible now and they are redesigning the site to meet that need (and, yes, if you can't tell, I'm very excited about that).

I recommend having a desk in your rental and setting your Airbnb listing inputs to reflect the dedicated workspace, but I also strongly encourage listing the highlights of your office space in the headline. Here are some examples:

- *Remote Worker Optimized Airbnb in the Heart of Downtown Denver*
- *Standing Desk and Second Screen Airbnb Remote Worker Haven*
- *Perfect for Remote Work Stays*
- *30+ Day Stays on the Beach*

One more thing that might interest you. I just did a little local research on properties that were pet-friendly and had a dedicated workspace that I could rent from June 3rd to September 30th and not even one had the words "Remote Worker" in the headline. I don't know about you, but that sounds like an opportunity to me! Here are some numbers showing how many places were available using that criteria.

Entire place, June 3rd – September 30th

	Pet-friendly + dedicated working space	Just dedicated working space	Just pet-friendly
Denver	75	260	85
Colorado Springs	8	47	16
Boise	17	54	28
Burlington	15	94	25
Austin	150	300+	184

Volume is both Airbnb's biggest advantage and disadvantage. More eyes mean more interest, which means more money. However, since you'll have more competition, it may be harder to stand out on Airbnb. Because some people still don't think of it as the go-to platform for 30+ day stays, you may have an advantage for the next six months to a year.

To summarize, the pros of using Airbnb are the volume, ease of use, and new functionality targeted toward workers seeking out 30+ day stays.

Now it's time to discuss the cons: the money, the third-party babysitting, the false sense of security with insurance, and the obnoxious algorithm.

While Airbnb's 3% charge feels modest, it is actually quite a bit higher than other services. For example, we rent out a three-bedroom, two-bathroom Denver condo for $3,000/month. Most of our tenants stay for two to four months. Our current tenants will have been in the space for eleven months when their lease ends. $3,000 x 11 = $33,000. 3% of $33,000 is $990. So, for the privilege of using Airbnb, I am paying nearly a grand. If this had been a rental that lasted three months, I'd still be paying $270. This is way more expensive than the other platforms, so it is something to consider. Because we know Airbnb has a higher volume, but also a bigger cut, you could raise the price more for your Airbnb listings.

When I say third-party babysitting, what I mean is that the contract is no longer 1:1 between yourself and the tenant. Airbnb is also involved, and a whole lot of people tend to think Airbnb is more lenient toward the tenant/guest than the landlord/host. I haven't had any negative experiences in this regard, but some of my clients have relayed this feedback. What this means is that there is no formalized lease outside of Airbnb and there is no immediate payment on the rent or deposit. If there is a disagreement between the two parties, Airbnb plays arbiter and, at the very least, involving them adds another layer of oversight.

Airbnb has Host Protection Insurance for up to one million dollars on listings. I get why they offer this, and it helped me feel better about renting my place to strangers, but you need a second insurance product on top of this. Why? Because if things go sideways and you need that insurance, Airbnb makes you file a claim with your home insurance before they will pay out. And since your home insurance is going to find out anyway and likely build your policy around that use, you may as well just tell them and be fully protected.

This is manageable. You just need to be transparent with your home insurance. They know more than you. They can outspend your life savings eight thousand times over just to protect themselves from future claims similar to yours. What I'm saying here is: you probably won't win. Tell them what you are doing. Most carriers have a short-term rental add-on to your home insurance; you pay a little more monthly for it, but you are covered. That said, be sure to tell them if you plan on 30+ day furnished rentals because often that will be a lower insurance rate than a short-term rental.

Finally, the pushy algorithm. I get it. It's effective. It's probably helpful. I just find Airbnb's automated emails to be obnoxious. Basically, you get hounded relentlessly via email, text, and every other means until you respond to an inquiring guest (serious or not) and the dopamine hit you get from Airbnb's attention soon morphs into digital annoyance. Airbnb has changed my life so positively that it's crazy I would ever complain about them, but here I am, complaining: their aggressive algorithm can be exhausting.

Furnished Finder

Furnished Finder is my favorite platform for sourcing remote workers. In their own words: "Furnished Finder is a short-term housing provider for travel nurses and other business travelers who need furnished housing. We boast a 92 day average stay, and are major data providers for corporate housing coordinators and medical staffing companies across the US. Property owners list their available short-term apartments on Furnished Finder, as healthcare travelers command a consistent appetite for traditional corporate housing and alternative housing types alike." This platform was built for people who wanted longer furnished stays and are professionally minded. In other words, the exact demographic we are pursuing.

Here's what I love about Furnished Finder: the price, the easy inputs, the lack of interest in reviews:

- The price: it's $99 for a year. Basically, if you plan on bringing in more than $3,333 in rents annually on your place, it's a better deal to use Furnished Finder than Airbnb. *That is so cheap*, and one day they will figure it out and raise rents on us, but until that day it's a great deal. And even on that day, it'll probably still be a great deal.
- It's easy to upload photos and inputs. There aren't many frills to this site, but it asks for everything you would want to share, and it doesn't stalk you relentlessly for the rest of your life.
- Nobody leaves reviews. If someone does, it's right there and you would see it, but very few people bother. It's great. As someone who knows a ton of hosts who worry about the difference between a four and five-star rating, it's nice to be on a platform where no one bothers.
- There isn't a ton of competition, so your listing, done properly, will really stand out.

Because Furnished Finder is not the most sophisticated platform, I recommend making yourself a strong communicator and a proactive host. This means that when a Furnished Finder request comes in, you respond in no less than twenty-four hours. You have a system that you walk tenants through so that they aren't floundering and confused about how to book or what comes next.

For our Furnished Finder tenants, we have the following process in place:

1. We respond to their email within twenty-four hours.
2. We end that email with this question: *Is there anything else we can help answer for you?* And this sentence: *If not, let us know and we'll start the application process.*
3. If they are ready to start the application process, we let them know:
   a. we are going to send them an application request from Apartments.com, which they will have to pay for and will pull their credit and background check
   b. we need links to their social accounts: Facebook and LinkedIn
   c. we will send over a formal lease and a request for deposit (via Venmo) once the rental application is complete
   d. the lease must be signed, and the deposit submitted within seventy-two hours to secure the rental
4. Once secured, we send them a welcome message that includes check-in info, HOA contact info,

door codes, and an overview of the rental conditions per the lease.

This works great. It helps set them at ease and prevents us from having to answer a lot of questions. The system gives them confidence your rental is legitimate. You outshine your competitors in a space where there is significant demand but not a ton of outstanding communication or clear processes.

Inquiries from Furnished Finder

	1 Bed/1 Bath	3 bed/2 bath
Dec 2020	5	0
Jan 2021	5	2
Feb 2021	0	5
Mar 2021	1	3
Apr 2021	10	10

Facebook Marketplace

Facebook Marketplace has given us the fewest leads, but I still put listings here since it has completely eclipsed Craigslist and will continue to replace it in markets where that hasn't happened yet. It's easy to use, there are 190 million US Facebook users, there's comfort in seeing your potential renter's photo, etc. If you haven't used Facebook Marketplace yet, it's good for a wide range of commerce: selling and buying furniture, researching rentals, finding tenants, etc.

Additionally, many cities have dedicated subletting groups on Facebook. You can request to join these subletting groups and post there as well. Like Craigslist, sometimes people act weird on Facebook or have hilarious expectations of what the rent price should be and/or how they advertise themselves, but it's still worth it to be on this platform.

The main things I like about Facebook Marketplace are: it's free, it's a site many people are already on, and it will likely continue to grow in the future.

VRBO

I recognize that some readers of this book will wonder why we don't discuss VRBO (Vacation Rentals by Owner, aka, HomeAway). I've never personally used or needed to use VRBO, so it's not something I can speak to nor is it a platform I've needed to keep my places rented. For that reason, I'm still not going to discuss VRBO.

Hailey + Gus | Minneapolis, MN | Remote Worker

Seeking two-bedroom or more rental in Texas, Denver, Seattle, Nashville, or Tucson for late summer 2021

How long are you traveling?

I think four months. We have a lease here until end of July, and we want to travel from the beginning of August through the end of November.

How long are you staying at each destination?

We are really set on spending two months in Seattle, and then one month each in some other locations.

Which platforms are you using?

We have been using Furnished Finder because we like it price wise, and [the] availability. We use Airbnb too, but the markup on prices makes it hard. Also, those people get better rates with nightly stays, so it is more expensive.

We've noticed a big price increase on Airbnb and VRBO since travel has started again.

What are your must haves?

We like to research neighborhoods. We want lots of things to do around us, like go to restaurants, go out at night every once in a while, shops, restaurants, bars, etc.

Space wise, especially working from home, having a spot for desks and not feeling too cramped is important. The most important thing to us is our proximity to things to do. We would not do a studio for this long of a stay. Extra amenities are good, but not necessary.

How old are you?

I'm twenty-three, and he's twenty-three.

What's your profession?

He works in consulting, and I am going to be in real estate.

.chapter ten.
Marketing Your Place

MARKETING IS EVERYTHING. It exists everywhere, and you do it a lot already, so embrace it. You market yourself when you go for a job interview or a date, you market your furniture when you list it on Facebook Marketplace, you market yourself when you buy clothes. Basically, you broadcast who you are to the world, but you tailor that broadcast to your audience. Case in point, when I used to be asked in job interviews in my twenties about weaknesses, I'd mention that I could be Type-A, which suggests I'm organized and will be quick to respond. That's true. Also true at that time in my life: *My Sunday day drinking with friends occasionally bled into the afternoon so sometimes I'd be hungover on Mondays.* I knew not to say that because I filtered the information based on my audience. The same principles apply to marketing your property.

Professional Photos

Professional photos are an obvious and easy place to start marketing your rental. This doesn't require much besides finding someone online (Google "professional real estate photos"). Depending on the size of the property, it will take between half an hour and three hours for the shoot, and the turnaround time should be fast. As this is their expertise, the photographer will know how to set lighting, what to keep or remove from the frame, etc. Outside of this, you just need to make sure that you have asked them to photograph the workspace so that your tenants know where the remote work will be getting done (And, yes, try to make that space look as nice and decluttered as possible. And, no, you should not be in these photos nor should anyone else).

Before you point your iPhone out to me and explain that you are part of the FIRE movement, let me assure you that professional photos will have one of the highest returns on investment of any decision in your life. I am in complete agreement that the iPhone takes a great shot. I am not in complete agreement that *you* take a great shot. Professional photos are so important that you don't want to mess them up.

In chapter four, we discussed how remote workers, like other renters, will be accessing a marketplace full of listings and the first decision they make will be based off the initial photo. As we covered there, that photo needs to be bright and look professional. You don't want your future tenant to have to strain to see what's in the photo, because they won't. They will just move to the next photo that is well-lit. Professional photos guarantee this piece gets done right.

The *Houzz* article also mentioned in chapter four emphasized that people like outdoor and kitchen photos best when selecting a place. I certainly think an outdoor photo is an appropriate first photo when marketing to remote workers. They are likely relocating to try out new weather or a new geography.

Headline

A strong headline addresses whoever your tenants may be and whatever they're looking for.

- *30+ Day, 1 bed/1 bath near Downtown*
- *Remote Work Residence in Highlands Neighborhood*
- *Parking/AC/Wi-Fi Studio in Hip Uptown*
- *Dishwasher/Laundry + Full Kitchen – 3/2*
- *Dishwasher/Laundry/Kitchen + Full Fence*
- *30+ Day Rental with Private Office with Second Screen for Remote Work*
- *High Speed Wi-Fi / 2 Bed with Private Office*
- *Pet-Friendly 3/2 with Fully Fenced Backyard Near Downtown*
  - o Did you know that Airbnb does not have any criteria for a fence for the guest to search? Adding this to your headline could be a huge help.

This is how you start advertising your rental, but over time, you'll also monitor what is showing up in reviews and (assuming they are positive and appropriate) reflect those details in the headline.

I had a client who kept getting amazing reviews about her game room and what a great hostess she was. I advised her to mention the game room in the headline since that was a differentiator for her property. Also, it's easy for people to see themselves enjoying ping pong with their family or putting a puzzle together. Mentioning games set the tone for family time.

While her wonderful personality also kept showing up in the reviews, I did not advise her to include that because most successful hosts show up in their own reviews as being very accommodating, professional, nice. For that reason, it's not a feature that would stand out.

Make It Easy

Make important information easy to find. This means using proper grammar, breaking different topics out into their own paragraphs, and putting a return space between those paragraphs. Doing this makes skimming your listing easy.

Additionally, answer questions for your guests before they ask. Think about what their concerns are and speak directly to them: note the Wi-Fi speed, call out the desk, advertise the second monitor, highlight the fully-enclosed fence, mention extra storage.

If you notice that the same question keeps coming up, incorporate the answer into your listing.

Part III | Logistics

There are some basic logistics for furnished rentals that are different than long-term rentals. We'll discuss what to charge remote workers, utilities, the cost of furniture, vacancies, and leases here.

.chapter eleven.
How Much Will Remote Workers Pay?

How Much Can You Charge Remote Workers?

Because 30+ day rentals do not start as year-long rentals (even if they occasionally do extend to year-long), they are affected by seasonality the same way hotels and standard Airbnbs are. This means that there will be higher demand and you will be able to charge a higher price during peak season (great weather, events, etc.) and a lower price during off season. I would anticipate charging approximately 25% less for off season than peak season. For us, this has meant getting $2,000/month on our one-bedroom condo in downtown Denver during peak season (April – October for Denver), and as low as $1,600/month on the same condo October-March.

You may also be curious about how much you can charge 30+ day remote workers compared to what you can charge long-term renters or short-term renters. Sales wise, assuming you are not using any property managers on the different properties, you will make the least with a long-term renter, the most with a short-term renter, and somewhere between the two with a remote worker paying medium-term renter prices.

A conservative estimate assumes that a property being used as a short-term rental will make twice as much as the same property being used as a long-term rental. So, if a property will make $1,000 per month long-term, it will make $2,000 per month on Airbnb. A good rule of thumb for what you can charge for the medium-term rate is 35-40% more than a long-term rental. So, on a $1,000 per month long-term rental property, you can assume you will make between $1,350-$1,400 per month doing medium-term rents.

I have an idea. Let's do a table again:

	Hypothetical rents on the same property	Multiplier
Long-term rents	$1,000/month	1
Medium-term rents	$1,350-$1,400/month	1.35-1.4
Short-term rents	$2,000/month	2

Other Costs

Furniture

You will have to factor furniture costs into your upfront investment. Note that the resell value of furniture is pretty low/nonexistent, so this will be a lost cost. These are rough numbers for buying basic, new furniture on different sized properties.

	Approximate Cost
Studio	$4,500
One Bedroom	$5,500
Two Bedrooms	$6,700
Three Bedrooms	$7,900

For each additional bedroom, we're factoring in a cost bump of approximately $1200, which includes a bed frame, a new queen mattress, two sets of queen sheets, a desk and a dresser.

My preference is to buy furniture on Amazon. They have a range of styles and prices. You can see reviews and photos of the product in other people's houses. The Amazon Best Seller tag makes it easy to pick out things you don't want to give much thought to (kitchenware, for example) and it all gets delivered to your house and can be scheduled. Added to all of that, if you put it on an Amazon card, you can get 5% back on all purchases.

Some of my clients (and occasionally, my husband) go the frugal route and source their furniture from the Salvation Army and Goodwill. I have heard, and I believe, that even after you rent a truck and ruin all your weekends and friendships by offering pizza in exchange for eight hours of moving, it is cheaper. I'm sure it is. *But* being on the hunt for the perfect couch at Goodwill seems like it will end with me just buying it off Amazon or at IKEA anyway, so I figure why not cut straight to the chase? As an added bonus, it's more time efficient to do it that way, which means you aren't also losing rental days and rental dollars.

Finally, the best/cheapest way to acquire furniture for your property is to offer to purchase the seller's furniture. They may be eager to buy new furniture for a new house as well as unenthused about moving cumbersome items. The hope is that will make them more willing to let it go for cheap and/or for free. If that pans out, it may be the cheapest way for you to source the furniture.

Utilities

Because there are different strategies for how to handle the utilities on a rental, let's discuss those, and the pros and cons associated with each one. But first, let's establish which utilities will need to be covered by you, the HOA, the tenant, or a blend of all the above.

Here are the utilities:

- Wi-Fi
- cable
- water
- heat (and possibly AC)
- yard maintenance
- snow removal

Strategy 1: Keep the utilities in your name + charge the tenants

I am listing this as the first strategy because it's the strategy my husband and I use with our tenants. This just makes transitioning from tenant to tenant easier, it's straightforward, and because we are lazy, this is how we do it.

The cost of certain utilities will change month to month (water, electricity). The way we've dealt with the cost is to take a deposit and then set the tenant on a budget based off what we agree is fair. If they go over that budget during their stay, we subtract that from the deposit. This is a little labor intensive as I feel to be fair you need to let them know what they've spent every month on utilities, so they can adjust.

Strategy 2: Let the tenants handle it

This might be easier for your bank account and your administrative maintenance, but it seems like a bad experience and one that tenants will balk at. When I'm traveling, I want to unpack, eat, and hit the beach. I do not want to unpack, get on the phone with Comcast, and not know when I'll be able to relax again because I'm still on hold after forty-five minutes.

Because remote worker renters are closer in mindset to short-term renters, I think they'll want an experience that makes their lives easy and will be willing to pay more for it. What that translates to is: you keep the utilities in your name, even if your ability to control water and gas is lost. Charge for these conveniences.

Smart Devices

Installing a smart thermostat for either scenario is recommended. It can help you and the tenant monitor energy use in real time and adjust as needed.

Vacancy Periods

Baking two-day vacancy periods into our turnovers helps us guarantee the property can be cleaned adequately. Occasionally, we bake slightly longer amounts of time into the turnover period if we believe we might like to use the property ourselves for a few days.

For the first two years that we ran our medium-term rentals, our average annual vacancy period on a 1/1 condo and a 3/2 condo was three weeks and five days, respectively. It is easier to shorten the vacancy during the summer season.

The holidays are when it has been hardest to find tenants and when we have had our longest stretches of vacancies. We have had to reduce our price by several hundred dollars per month to cover the period between November through early February.

Now that we've identified this pattern, we are working harder to find tenants who can stay through this season to avoid these vacancies. Should that not work, we will make our November contracts shorter so that we do not have the reduced rental rate long-term.

The holidays are also a time of year when people doing Airbnb have issues getting consistent, high-paying bookings. For this reason, a lot of Airbnb hosts actually move to remote worker/medium-term rentals during the holidays. It helps them cover the period when there is limited interest without requiring much work.

Remote Worker / Medium-Term Leases

Medium-term describe the length of the lease; the term *remote worker* describes who you aspire to lease to. The lease you use for a remote worker is the same lease you would use for anyone hoping to rent your furnished property for 30+ days.

I recommend having a welcome sheet that covers the details of the lease and the unit with your tenants.

The first part of the welcome sheet should include standard rent info: what the deposit is, what the cleaning deposit is, what the pet rental rate is, what the rent amount is, when the rent is due, what the move in/move out dates are, how and where to pay rent, etc. None of that is too interesting or unique to medium-term rentals.

What is unique to medium-term rentals is the renewal period. Remote workers have a lot of flexibility, and they often get complacent. If they have enjoyed the lifestyle and have gotten their bearings in your city, they might not be eager to move. That's great, and retaining your existing renter (if you've liked them) should be a priority—no lost cost or time acquiring a new tenant. If they decide to renew, you review the lease and confirm that the price you have been charging them is competitive with the season you are entering. If they have been paying an increased rate through the summer and are willing to continue to pay that increased rate through the late fall/winter, great. Keep them. However, if you acquired them late fall/winter and had reduced the rate to secure them, the lease needs to be revisited. If they want to stay, you can either increase the price or accept the reduced rate because you like the tenant more than you want the extra money.

We ask our tenants if they want to renew at the forty-five-day mark. The reason for this is to give us adequate time to relist the property and to secure another renter. It helps narrow the turnover window and prevents lost income from gaps in stay.

.chapter twelve.
Other Renter Types

While the focus of this book has been the emerging remote worker and what they need, this model also works for several other renter demographics. Beyond remote workers, a furnished 30+ day rental has historically been attractive to:

- traveling nurses
- corporate professionals, also called "executive rentals"
- people who are considering a divorce and need a month or so break to figure out next steps
- people who intend to purchase in the area but want to learn more about city neighborhoods they like before committing

I mention these subtypes because it will always be to your advantage to expand the pool of tenants you can rent to. While traveling nurses may be less concerned about Wi-Fi speed and having a home office, they have disposable income and need furnished units. Corporate and executive renters are the original remote worker. And people who need space from their spouse and/or are new to town also have the need for furnished rentals.

.chapter thirteen.
Revisiting the Future

As I write the final pages of this book, the United States has made COVID-19 vaccine available to anyone who wants it. While companies attempt to establish policies for the future, it is assumed that most employees will return to the office in a hybrid model: two-to-three days off site and/or the inverse, two-to-three days on site. Some companies have gone full remote long-term, but that is not the norm *just yet*.

This begs the question: Is the explosive movement of remote workers really going to happen? I still believe it is. According to *Gallup*, close to 66% of people who have been remote working would like to continue to do so as of October 2020. Half of those want to continue to work remotely because of COVID fears, and half of them again want to continue to work remotely because they like it.[lxxix] Further, current commute times in America are thirty minutes on average,[lxxx] and commute trends will worsen if we continue to make everyone report to the office five days a week.

I believe that people who have become accustomed to working remotely will be less interested in returning to the office and view it as an interruption of life and schedule. People like routine, and splitting time between spaces interrupts that routine. Now that the experiment has proven remote work can be done successfully by a large population, workers are better positioned to demand it. For that reason, I believe this phenomenon will grow massively over the next one-to-five years as we collect ourselves and re-establish the new normal.

Equally important is what motivates the employer. Some studies show remote workers are 1.4 days per week more productive than their peers,[lxxxi] and it is estimated that remote work is saving employers $22,000 per year, per employee.[lxxxii] If that trend continues, employers will be motivated to keep employees remote.

If you believe technology giants are visionaries, then you should believe permanent, full-time remote work is coming. As of January 2021, Facebook is allowing strong performers in senior positions to apply for full-time remote work and is planning on allowing 50% of their 45,000-person staff to work remotely full time.[lxxxiii] Coinbase, Twitter, and Shopify have already adopted full-time remote work policies. Again, when considering if this trend is going to stick, we should look at who is doing it and why: full-time work saves these companies money, allows them to diversify their employment base, and potentially lowers salary obligations. That's a lot of incentive to keep people remote.

Part IV | Conclusion

When the option to do part-time work was first offered to me, I was excited about the opportunity, but I recognized from my boss's comments that it might be held against me. He offered this option because he felt it was necessary to acquire competitive talent but he preferred employees worked on site. While I understood it might hurt my long-term trajectory at the company, I considered remote work a major job perk and fully embraced working from home one day a week. Not only did I enjoy the break from office politics, I also got more work done from home.

For the next five years, I worked in middle management across three different companies, and while remote work was offered in a part-time capacity at every position, it remained a controversial topic in management meetings. Everyone my age or younger wanted it. Everyone older than me had trouble accepting it.

Around this time, I went into real estate, worked for myself, and worked full time from home. When COVID-19 started, I had been doing this for several years. I have zero intentions of returning to work for someone else, but if I did, remote work would be non-negotiable. I would not take any job that required me to return to an office. I feel strongly about this for a few reasons. The first is that I consider my time to be my most valuable asset, and if I have to work for someone else, working remotely at least somewhat helps me protect that asset. Second, because I don't work in an occupation that requires face-to-face contact, there is no need for me to be on site. I would question any employer who forced that. Does my employer feel that way because they don't trust their employees? Because they don't trust technology? Because they are married to the past? To me, any of these characteristics indicate an employer is a bad fit. And since it is estimated that 30% of the US workforce plans on quitting if they must return to an office,[lxxxiv] I know I'm not the only one who feels strongly about this subject.

For some of us, 2020 created an opportunity to reflect on who we have been and how we want the future to be different. Sometimes that is easy to figure out and sometimes it is not. Personally, it reminded me of the decision my husband and I made to not have kids, and my feelings around that. Making that choice helped me feel more confident I could quit my job and try being my own boss. (And, yes, I recognize you can quit your job if you have kids. If you do, my hat is off to you. I am only making this point to acknowledge that, in my opinion, being childless reduces the stakes when quitting your job.) My point is, I felt that not having kids freed up a lot of opportunities and I needed to fully take advantage of that.

While my epiphany around not having kids and starting my own business happened years before

COVID-19 took root, once everyone was locked down, I imagined that people who were lucky enough to just be bored (versus unemployed, sick, worried, or grieving) might also be thinking about a different future. It seemed logical that no longer being geographically tethered to your job would factor into that reflection. From that point forward, I started tracking articles on remote workers and thinking about how this shift would impact my profession (real estate). This book is the result of those thoughts.

I love real estate because it allowed me to become my own boss and recoup my time. Many of the people I work with are investors and feel the same way. They don't necessarily have a passion for owning real estate; they have a passion for the personal freedom that comes with being your own boss. They view real estate as the fastest path to reach that freedom.

I know this sounds cheesy but having control over how to spend my day is monumental. My time means more to me than any paycheck, and working in a career where I have control and I am happy is much more lucrative than working for someone else.

While this book is about how to identify, target, and convert remote workers into tenants, I hope it also helps you think about how the future will be different. 2020 was a tough year, but if it allowed you the luxury of reflection, it's time to think about how this experience could shake things up, and how to make that work for you.

Thank you for reading my book. Sincerely, thank you. It's been a lifelong dream of mine to write one and I'm very proud to have completed it and flattered that you read it.

If you have questions about real estate or remote workers as tenants, please feel free to email me at Erin@AmericanNomadsBook.com. I am still accepting clients and promise I always respond to emails.

Part V | Checklists

Please believe me when I say that checklists can save you time and headaches. I know, they feel redundant. They feel annoying. And they feel like something you know you should do but you don't want to do. Trust me: you should. Checklists are the difference between one trip to IKEA and four trips to IKEA.

Your Listing

You might not have some of the items below (like parking), and that's fine, but don't make your future tenant dig for this information. Give it to them up front.

o   Professional photos
- ❏   Make your primary photo an outdoor space, a kitchen space, or a well-organized and cute office
- ❏   Remove personal photos from fridge/tables/walls for photos
- ❏   Remove art from the walls for photos
- ❏   No humans should be in the photos
- ❏   Remove or hide about one third of your furniture

o   Your headline should advertise what makes you different
- ❏   Pet-friendly
- ❏   Putting "Remote Worker Haven" in headline
- ❏   Fence or dog door
- ❏   Desk, standing desk, or second screen
- ❏   AC
- ❏   Parking
- ❏   Laundry on site

o   If not in the headline, then in the body of the listing, you should include:
- ❏   A fence
- ❏   Dishwasher
- ❏   AC
- ❏   A dog door

- ❑ On site laundry
- ❑ Covered or heated parking
- ❑ What you love about it
- ❑ Wi-Fi speed
- ❑ Parking
- ❑ Outdoor space
- ❑ Pet-friendly or unfriendly
  - ❑ If pet fees are charged
  - ❑ What that charge is
- ❑ Smoking friendly or unfriendly
- ❑ A note that these are for 30+ day rentals
- ❑ Office perks if you have them:
  - ❑ Office space
  - ❑ Private or quiet rooms
  - ❑ Desks
  - ❑ Standing desks
  - ❑ Second screen monitor
  - ❑ Wi-Fi speed

- o If you have a:
  - ❑ Game room
  - ❑ Pool
  - ❑ Sauna
  - ❑ Hot tub

- o Your proximity to:
  - ❑ Hospitals
  - ❑ Colleges
  - ❑ Recreation
  - ❑ City centers
  - ❑ Public transportation

Furnished Finder Intake

- ❏ Timely email response
- ❏ Question about what else you can answer for them or next steps
- ❏ Next steps
    - ❏ Background check
    - ❏ Credit check
    - ❏ Social accounts
- ❏ Lease
- ❏ Deposit
- ❏ Cancellation Policy
- ❏ Timeline for completed lease and deposit
- ❏ Welcome materials
    - ❏ Contact info
    - ❏ Lease details
    - ❏ Access codes
        - ❏ Building
        - ❏ Unit
        - ❏ Laundry
        - ❏ Gym
        - ❏ Mail

Your Lease

- ❏ Price
- ❏ Length
- ❏ If the property is under an LLC, the lease is between the tenant and the LLC
- ❏ Proper notice for entering
- ❏ Proper notice for showing the place
- ❏ Proper notice for when and if they want to renew
- ❏ Cleaning fee
- ❏ How to pay (Venmo, personal check, bank withdrawal, etc.)
- ❏ Who is responsible for maintenance
- ❏ Responsibility and expectations around yard work
- ❏ Responsibility and expectations around snow shoveling
- ❏ Subleasing: allowing or not allowing for Airbnb, etc. if tenant leaves for weekend or longer
- ❏ Guests: when you would need to be notified if someone is staying there who is not on the lease
- ❏ Lists of your furniture and items
- ❏ Video documentation of the property

Utilities

- ❏ Trash
- ❏ Water
- ❏ Gas
- ❏ Electricity
- ❏ Wi-Fi
- ❏ Cable

Bedroom

- ❏ Hangers
- ❏ Queen or King mattress
- ❏ Queen or King bed
- ❏ 2 sets of sheets
- ❏ Duvet or Comforter
- ❏ 2 pillows
- ❏ Lighting
- ❏ Bedside table
- ❏ Power strip for charging
- ❏ Full length mirror

Kitchen

- ❏ 8 forks
- ❏ 8 knives
- ❏ 8 spoons
- ❏ 8 plates
- ❏ 8 water glasses
- ❏ 2 mugs per bedroom
- ❏ Coffee maker
- ❏ Pan set
- ❏ Baking set
- ❏ Utensils
  - ❏ Spatula
  - ❏ Tongs

- ❏ Scissors
- ❏ Large sharp knife
- ❏ Large, serrated knife
- ❏ Smaller paring knife
- ❏ Two cutting boards
- ❏ Soup pot
- ❏ Basic spices
- ❏ Kitchen towels

Bathroom

- ❏ 2 towels per person
- ❏ Hand towel
- ❏ Sink towel
- ❏ Bath mat
- ❏ Soap dish tray
- ❏ Toothpaste/toothbrush cup
- ❏ Hair catcher for the drain

Living Room

- ❏ Couch
- ❏ Portable desk stands
- ❏ Television (40+ inches)
- ❏ Coffee table
- ❏ Lights (either overhead or as lamps)
- ❏ Throw blanket
- ❏ Smart thermostat

Outdoor

- ❏ White lights
- ❏ Grill
- ❏ Firepit
- ❏ Furniture
- ❏ Xeriscaped to some degree
- ❏ Fence
- ❏ Lawn mower
- ❏ Snow shovel
- ❏ Rake
- ❏ Garden hose
- ❏ Outside dining table and chairs and/or outdoor couch
- ❏ Smart lock

Office

- ❏ Desk
- ❏ Multiple surge protectors
- ❏ Desk lamp
- ❏ Desk chair
- ❏ Second screen
- ❏ Power strips
- ❏ White board
- ❏ Stapler
- ❏ Scissors
- ❏ Cheap paper pads
- ❏ Bookcase or shelving
- ❏ Pens
- ❏ White noise machine

What Your Tenants Will Need to Know Once They've Arrived

❏   The Wi-Fi name and password
❏   Contact information for you: email and phone
❏   Contact information for the landlord or building supervisor
❏   Any door codes they may need
    o   For entering the unit
    o   Exterior Access (condos)
    o   Gym/Laundry/Pool/Trash access (condos)
    o   Padlock on the back shed
❏   Parking space location or number
❏   Storage space location or number

Part VI | References

i "Airbnb: Nearly 25% of Guests Booked Stays of 28 days or Longer", Christina Jelski, Travel Weekly, May 2021, https://www.travelweekly.com/Travel-News/Hotel-News/Airbnb-said-quarter-of-guests-booked-long-stays

ii "Now That More Americans Can Work From Anywhere, Many Are Planning to Move Away", Adedayo Akala, NPR, October 2020, https://www.npr.org/sections/coronavirus-live-updates/2020/10/30/929667563/now-that-more-americans-can-work-anywhere-many-are-planning-to-move-away

iii "25+ Digital Nomad Statistics and Trends in 2021" Sarah Archer, Anyplace, October 2020, https://www.anyplace.com/blog/digital-nomad-statistics/

iv "'The DNA of Work has Changed' Many Americans want to keep working from home after the COVID-19 crisis passes" Paul Davidson, USA Today, May 2021. https://www.usatoday.com/story/money/2021/05/19/work-home-covid-many-people-want-keep-working-remotely/5150568001/

v "The Top 10 U.S. Metros for Digital Nomads" Zillow Research, April 2021, https://www.zillow.com/research/digital-nomads-zillow-yelp-2021-29393/?utm_source=email&utm_medium=email&utm_campaign=emm_zg_g_buzzvaccinemoving_050821_1_national_rng_21brand_emm&utm_content=digitalnomadcta

vi "Remote work statistics: Navigating the New Normal" Emily Courtney, Flexjobs, December 2020, https://www.flexjobs.com/blog/post/remote-work-statistics/

vii "How longer stays can help your hosting business right now" Airbnb, Sept 2020, https://www.airbnb.com/resources/hosting-homes/a/how-longer-stays-can-help-your-hosting-business-right-now-182

viii "Thinking of making a move? Try out a new city with Airbnb." Airbnb, May 2021, https://news.airbnb.com/thinking-of-making-a-move-try-out-a-new-city-with-airbnb/

ix "COVID-19 and Remote Work: An Update", Megan Brenan, Gallup, October 2020, https://news.gallup.com/poll/321800/covid-remote-work-update.aspx#:~:text=Currently%2C%2033%25%20are%20always%20working,2.

x "COVID-19 and Remote Work: An Update", Megan Brenan, Gallup, October 2020, https://news.gallup.com/poll/321800/covid-remote-work-update.aspx#:~:text=Currently%2C%2033%25%20are%20always%20working,2.

xi "Airbnb: Remote Workers could spur new kind of business travel" Donna M. Airoldi, Business Travel News, May 2021, https://www.businesstravelnews.com/Lodging/Airbnb-Remote-Workers-Could-Spur-New-Kind-of-Business-Travel

xii "Working from Home Increases Productivity" Sammi Caramela, Business News Daily, March 2020, https://www.businessnewsdaily.com/15259-working-from-home-more-productive.html#:~:text=Working%20From%20Home%20Increases%20Productivity&text=According%20to%20one%20study%2C%20remote,weeks%20of%20work%20per%20year.

xiii "Nearly a third of workers don't want to ever return to the office" Lance Lambert, Fortune, December 2020, https://fortune.com/2020/12/06/offices-covid-workers-returning-never-want-to-stats-data-2/

xiv "Facebook is the latest major tech company to let people work from home forever" Shirin Ghaffary, Vox, May 2020, https://www.vox.com/recode/2020/5/21/21266570/facebook-remote-work-from-home-mark-zuckerberg-twitter-covid-19-coronavirus

xv "Facebook is the latest major tech company to let people work from home forever" Shirin Ghaffary, Vox, May 2020, https://www.vox.com/recode/2020/5/21/21266570/facebook-remote-work-from-home-mark-zuckerberg-twitter-covid-19-coronavirus

xvi "31% of young adults relocated during Covid." Lorie Konish, CNBC, March 2021, https://www.cnbc.com/2021/03/15/31percent-of-young-adults-moved-during-covid-what-that-means-for-cities.html

xvii "Wikipedia: Digital Nomad" *Wikipedia*, April 2021, https://en.wikipedia.org/wiki/Digital_nomad

xviii "What's Next for Remote Work" Susan Lund, Anu Madgavkar, James Manyika and Sven Smit, McKinsey Global Institute, November 2020, https://www.mckinsey.com/featured-insights/future-of-work/whats-next-for-remote-work-an-analysis-of-2000-tasks-800-jobs-and-nine-countries#

xix "Remote Work from Home Salary" ZipRecruiter, https://www.ziprecruiter.com/Salaries/Remote-Work-From-Home-Salary

xx "Rule of Thumb: How Much Should You Spend on Rent?" Rebecca Lake, The Balance, April 2021, https://www.thebalance.com/what-percentage-of-your-income-should-go-to-rent-4688840

xxi "Remote Work from Home Salary" ZipRecruiter, https://www.ziprecruiter.com/Salaries/Remote-Work-From-Home-Salary

xxii "2021 US Tax Calculator" iCalculator, May 2021,
https://us.icalculator.info/salary-illustration/66000.html

xxiii "Some cities are paying people up to $16,000 to move there"
Jennifer Liu, CNBC make it, March 2021,
https://www.cnbc.com/2021/03/16/makemymove-online-
directory-of-cities-that-pay-you-to-move-there.html

xxiv "25+ Digital Nomad Statistics and Trends in 2021" Sarah
Archer, Anyplace, October 20, 2020,
https://www.anyplace.com/blog/digital-nomad-statistics/

xxv "Women in the Workplace 2020", Sarah Coury, Jess Huang,
Ankur Kumar, Sara Prince, Alexis Krivkovich, Lareina Yee,
McKinsey & Company, September 2020.

xxvi "Do Women Take As Many Risks as Men?" Doug Sundheim,
Harvard Business Review, February 2013,
https://hbr.org/2013/02/do-women-take-as-many-risks-as

xxvii "More than Walls Separate Male, Female Tenants" Bill
Brashler, Chicago Tribune, June 1999,
https://www.chicagotribune.com/news/ct-xpm-1999-06-23-
9906230302-story.html

xxviii "Sexes Sense of Security" Farh and Farah,
https://farahandfarah.com/studies/sexes-sense-of-safety/

xxix "More than Walls Separate Male, Female Tenants" Bill
Brashler, Chicago Tribune, June 1999,
https://www.chicagotribune.com/news/ct-xpm-1999-06-23-
9906230302-story.html

xxx "More than Walls Separate Male, Female Tenants" Bill Brashler,
Chicago Tribune, June 1999,
https://www.chicagotribune.com/news/ct-xpm-1999-06-23-
9906230302-story.html

xxxi "Females find social interactions to be more rewarding than
males, study finds" Science Daily, Georgia State University, January

2019, https://www.sciencedaily.com/releases/2019/01/190130175604.htm

xxxii "Raising Children in the Early 17th Century: Demographics" Plymouth Ancestors, https://www.plimoth.org/sites/default/files/media/pdf/edmaterials_demographics.pdf

xxxiii "Too Old To be a Nomad? Think Again" Sean Clark, Krisp, Feb 2020, https://krisp.ai/blog/never-old-to-be-a-nomad/#:~:text=Most%20Digital%20Nomads%20Are%20Older%20than%20the%20Stereotype&text=According%20to%20a%20survey%20by,of%20nomads%20are%20over%2038.

xxxiv "Digitial Nomad Infographic" Katherine Conaway, Digital Nomad Survival Guide, May 2017, https://medium.com/digital-nomad-survival-guide/digital-nomad-infographic-case-study-d30a3a646dac

xxxv "31% of Young Adults Relocated During Covid" Lorie Konish, CNBC, Mar 2021, https://www.cnbc.com/2021/03/15/31percent-of-young-adults-moved-during-covid-what-that-means-for-cities.html

xxxvi "10 Most Expensive U.S. Cities to Live in for 2020" Education Loan Finance, Kat Tretina, March 2020, https://www.elfi.com/10-most-expensive-us-cities-to-live-in-for-2020/

xxxvii "The 20 Most Expensive Cities in the U.S." Kiplingers, Dan Burrows, July 2020, https://www.kiplinger.com/real-estate/601142/20-most-expensive-cities-in-the-us

xxxviii "Tony Robbins Explains One Way to Save Major Money", Insider, Tony Robbins, January 2015, https://www.businessinsider.com/tony-robbins-explains-one-way-to-save-major-money-2015-1

xxxix "Every state, Ranked by How Miserable Its Winters Are" Matt Lynch, Thrillist, October 2020,

https://www.thrillist.com/travel/nation/states-with-the-worst-winters-worst-us-states-for-winter

xl "Every state, Ranked by How Miserable Its Winters Are" Matt Lynch, Thrillist, October 2020, https://www.thrillist.com/travel/nation/states-with-the-worst-winters-worst-us-states-for-winter

xli "How to Recognize Valuable Traits in Remote Workers" Sally Norton, PR-News, January 2021, https://www.agilitypr.com/pr-news/public-relations/how-to-recognize-valuable-traits-in-remote-workers/

xlii "Attract New Tenants with Technology" Lauren Mason, Buildium, July 2017, https://www.buildium.com/blog/attract-new-tenants-with-technology/

xliii "They Can't Leave the Bay Area Fast Enough" Nellie Bowles, The New York Times, January 2021, https://www.nytimes.com/2021/01/14/technology/san-francisco-covid-work-moving.html

xliv "Working from Home: The Office Will Never be the Same" Claire Cain Miller, The New York Times, August 2020, https://www.nytimes.com/2020/08/20/style/office-culture.html

xlv "List of United States cities by population" *Wikipedia*, April 2021, https://en.wikipedia.org/wiki/List_of_United_States_cities_by_population

xlvi "Tulsa Remote and Airbnb help Remote Workers 'try before they buy' in Tulsa", Airbnb, Feb 2021, https://news.airbnb.com/tulsa-remote-and-airbnb-help-remote-workers-try-before-they-buy-in-tulsa/

xlvii "More Single American Opting to Own Pets" Veterinary Practice News, March 2013, https://www.veterinarypracticenews.com/more-single-americans-opting-to-own-pets-avma-study-discovers/#:~:text=Pet%20ownership%20among%20divorced%2C%20widowed,from%2051.3%20to%2060.4%20percent.&text=The%20number%20of%20single%20men,from%2034.3%20to%2043.8%20perc

ent.&text=The%20number%20of%20single%20women,from%2046.8
%20to%2057.1%20percent.

xlviii "Why you should consider a pet-friendly Airbnb" Katie
Reeves, Mashvisor, January 2020.
https://www.mashvisor.com/blog/pet-friendly-
airbnb/#:~:text=On%20average%2C%20only%20three%20percent,a
%20pet%2Dfriendly%20Airbnb%20accommodation.

xlix "5 Reasons You Should Allow Pets at Your Rental Property"
Kaycee Miller, Rentec Direct, March 2017,
https://www.rentecdirect.com/blog/5-reasons-allow-pets-rental-
property/

l "Study: 66% of Remote Workers print work-related documents at
home", Michael Hill, Info Security Group, January 2021,
https://www.infosecurity-magazine.com/news/workers-printing-
docs-home/

li "New insights into how guests are using Airbnb for longer term
stays" Airbnb, November 2020, https://news.airbnb.com/new-
insights-into-how-guests-are-using-airbnb-for-longer-term-stays/

lii "New insights into how guests are using Airbnb for longer term
stays" Airbnb, November 2020, https://news.airbnb.com/new-
insights-into-how-guests-are-using-airbnb-for-longer-term-stays/

liii "Male v. Female Car Insurance Rates" Ava Lynch, The Zebra,
April 2021, https://www.thezebra.com/auto-
insurance/driver/other-factors/male-vs-female-car-insurance-
rates/

liv "Sexes Sense of Security" Farah and Farah,
https://farahandfarah.com/studies/sexes-sense-of-safety/

lv "Sexes Sense of Security" Farah and Farah,
https://farahandfarah.com/studies/sexes-sense-of-safety/

lvi "13 Best Ways to Add Value" Jennifer Ebert, Home & Gardens, January 2021, https://www.homesandgardens.com/news/best-ways-to-add-value-home

lvii "15 All-Time-Favorite *Houzz* Photos Shared by Readers" Bryan Anthony, *Houzz*, October 2020, https://www.houzz.com/magazine/15-all-time-favorite-houzz-photos-shared-by-readers-stsetivw-vs~142380539

lviii "Share of Sports fans in the United States as of March 2021, by gender" Statista, March 2021, https://www.statista.com/statistics/1018814/sports-fans-usa-gender/

lix "Why has Covid-19 been especially harmful for working women?" Nicole Bateman and Martha Ross, Brookings, October 2020, https://www.brookings.edu/essay/why-has-covid-19-been-especially-harmful-for-working-women/

lx "Millennials" *Wikipedia*, May 2021, https://en.wikipedia.org/w/index.php?title=Millennials&action=history

lxi "Millennials" *Wikipedia*, April 2021, https://en.wikipedia.org/wiki/Millennials#:~:text=Date%20and%20age%20range%20definitions,-Oxford%20Living%20Dictionaries&text=According%20to%20this%20definition%2C%20the,25%20years%20old%20in%202021.

lxii "Generation-Z" *Wikipedia*, May 2021, https://en.wikipedia.org/wiki/Generation_Z

lxiii "Marion Remote Set to Lure Workers Here" Tina Shaw, Times West Virginian, January 2021, https://www.timeswv.com/community/community_columns/marion-remote-set-to-lure-remote-workers-here/article_b14dd976-5db6-11eb-9296-9bd4bd9fd0c0.html

lxiv "Some cities are paying people up to $16,000 to move there" Jennifer Liu, CNBC make it, March 2021,

https://www.cnbc.com/2021/03/16/makemymove-online-directory-of-cities-that-pay-you-to-move-there.html

lxv "Remote Work Statistics: Navigating the New Normal" Emily Courtney, Flexjobs, December 2020, https://www.flexjobs.com/blog/post/remote-work-statistics/

lxvi "People who work from home earn more than those that commute. Here's Why." Abigal Johnson Hess, CNBC Makeit, October 2019, https://www.cnbc.com/2019/10/13/people-who-work-from-home-earn-more-than-those-who-commuteheres-why.html

lxvii "Average Rent in Denver" Zumper, April 2021, https://www.zumper.com/rent-research/denver-co

lxviii "Average Rent in Tulsa" Zumper, April 2021, https://www.zumper.com/rent-research/tulsa-ok

lxix "Infographic. Which markets have the most full-time remote workers?" Brie Weiler Reynolds, Flexjobs, January 2018, https://www.flexjobs.com/blog/post/infographic-which-states-have-most-full-time-telecommuters/

lxx "Colorado to gain its first new congressional district in 20 years, but where yet to be determined." Justin Wingerter, The Denver Post, April 2021, https://www.denverpost.com/2021/04/26/colorado-congressional-district-8th-u-s-house-seat/

lxxi "Small Cities are a Big Draw for Remote Workers during the Pandemic" Jon Marcus, NPR, November 2020, https://www.npr.org/2020/11/16/931400786/small-cities-are-a-big-draw-for-remote-workers-during-the-pandemic#:~:text More%20young%2C%20well%2Dpaid%20and,a%20population%20just%20under%2043%2C000.

lxxii "Tony Robins Explains One Way to Save Major Money" Tony Robbins, Business Insider, January 2015,

https://www.businessinsider.com/tony-robbins-explains-one-way-to-save-major-money-2015-1

lxxiii "The Top 10 U.S. Metros for Digital Nomads" Zillow Research, April 2021, https://www.zillow.com/research/digital-nomads-zillow-yelp-2021-29393/?utm_source=email&utm_medium=email&utm_campaign=e mm_zg_g_buzzvaccinemoving_050821_1_national_rng_21brand_e mm&utm_content=digitalnomadcta

lxxiv "Tips for Soundproofing Your Home Office" Glenda Taylor, Bob Vila, https://www.bobvila.com/slideshow/10-tips-for-soundproofing-your-home-office-265365

lxxv *Optimize Your BNB: The Definitive Guide to Ranking #1 in Airbnb*, Daniel Vroman, January 2018, https://www.amazon.com/Optimize-Your-Airbnb-Definitive-Ranking/dp/099971550X

lxxvi "Airbnb: number of users in the United States from 2016 – 2022" S. Lock, Statista, Aug 2019, https://www.statista.com/statistics/346589/number-of-us-airbnb-users/

lxxvii "Airbnb just debuted on Wall Street." Sara O'Brien and Kaya Yurieff, CNN Business, December 2020, https://www.cnn.com/2020/12/10/tech/airbnb-ipo/index.html

lxxviii "Introducing 100 plus new upgrades to our service" Airbnb, Brian Chesky, May 2021, https://www.airbnb.com/2021

lxxix "COVID-19 and Remote Work: An Update", Megan Brenan, Gallup, October 2020, https://news.gallup.com/poll/321800/covid-remote-work-update.aspx#:~:text=Currently%2C%2033%25%20are%20always%20working,2.

lxxx "Working from Home Increases Productivity" Sammi Caramela, Business News Daily, March 2020, https://www.businessnewsdaily.com/15259-working-from-home-more-

productive.html#:~:text=Working%20From%20Home%20Increases
%20Productivity&text=According%20to%20one%20study%2C%20r
emote,weeks%20of%20work%20per%20year.

lxxxi "Working from Home Increases Productivity" Sammi
Caramela, Business News Daily, March 2020,
https://www.businessnewsdaily.com/15259-working-from-home-
more-
productive.html#:~:text=Working%20From%20Home%20Increases
%20Productivity&text=According%20to%20one%20study%2C%20r
emote,weeks%20of%20work%20per%20year.

lxxxii "In Defense of Remote Work" Jeff DeVerter, Forbes,
December 2020,
https://www.forbes.com/sites/forbestechcouncil/2020/12/02/in-
defense-of-remote-work/?sh=1cde34ac144a

lxxxiii "Facebook is the latest major tech company to let people
work from home forever" Shirin Ghaffary, Vox, May 2020,
https://www.vox.com/recode/2020/5/21/21266570/facebook-
remote-work-from-home-mark-zuckerberg-twitter-covid-19-
coronavirus

lxxxiv "Nearly 30% of working professionals would quit if they had
to return to office after pandemic" Paul Davidson, USA Today,
January 2021,
https://www.usatoday.com/story/money/2021/01/05/jobs-
home-29-professionals-would-quit-if-forced-go-back-
office/4142830001/